FELT FRIENDS

Beginner-Friendly Sewing Patterns
to Bring Kenneth Grahame's
Classic Tale to Life

Cynthia Treen

DAVID & CHARLES
—PUBLISHING—

www.davidandcharles.com

Contents

DEDICATION

*With boundless gratitude to my makers,
those who are and those yet to be! May we
continue to learn from each other.*

Introduction

Kenneth Grahame's classic story, with its unforgettable River Bank characters, is one of the joys of children's literature. *The Wind in the Willows* is a book filled with the sweet scent of meadow flowers and the seasons passing slowly, with kindness, friendship, loyalty, and adventure. The stories grew from Grahame's relationship with his son, Alastair, and they embody a gentle nostalgia to which we, in adulthood, can all relate.

For so many, the stories of Mole and Ratty, Badger and Toad, the River Bank, and the Wild Wood wove themselves into our childhood landscapes and imaginations. Now, with me guiding you every step of the way through these projects, you can bring the characters and settings to life in a new, dimensional way (their limbs are even designed to be posable, making them even more enchanting!). The characters are for everyone, those who grew up with them and those yet to discover and build on their adventures.

Whether you're a beginner or a seasoned stitcher, this book is for you. I love to learn myself, so I write and design for beginners, starting from the ground up with basic hand-stitching techniques, helpful tips, and lots of detail to guide you step-by-step through the process.

Some of you might be worried about making mistakes. I've always felt that the word "mistake" was an unfortunate word for opportunity! If you enjoy making, never be discouraged. Embrace mistakes and know their potential. When I first tried spinning at a wool fair, the kindly instructor told me before I began that whatever I made on my first spin, I must save forever. As my skill increased, she said I might never create something more wild or beautiful, and she was right! I still have that lovely bit of fiber, and I often think of her wise words. Experienced stitchers know this, but it bears repeating. My advice for the beginners in our midst is to be kind to yourself. Take your time. Know mistakes for what they are, make adjustments, and move forward with enjoyment. Experience has told me that first-time makers usually surprise themselves and are thrilled with their creations!

I believe that what Ratty said about living by the river applies to all creative endeavors:

"The times we've had together! Whether in winter or summer, spring or autumn, it's always got its fun and its excitements!"

And of course, feel free to improvise! Later in the book, you'll find inspiration and a rainbow of ideas to start making these characters truly yours.

My hope in recreating Kenneth Grahame's iconic characters in wool felt is that stitching them will make you as happy as it has me.

May you enjoy every moment of making and sharing your creations!

How to use this book

From choosing tools and making the characters to creating their little wardrobes and adorable accessories, I've planned our journey to be as easy (and picturesque!) as possible.

As you embark on the projects, you'll find useful advice in **Before You Begin**. **Tools & Materials** introduces the **Basic Sewing Kit** for working with felt, as well as the **Creative Materials** themselves.

The **Basic Body** section is your starting point for the characters—you'll discover which patterns you need, as well as stitching instructions. When making the outfits, you'll be asked to refer back to the **Basic Jacket** and **Basic Pants** sections for the foundations of the clothes. The project itself will help you select felt and notions. **Adding Details** has ideas for adapting the clothes to create additional styles and garments. No matter what your skill level and experience, the **Basic Techniques** section is there for you every step of the way.

If you or someone you know owns a traditional 1:12 scale dollhouse, you might want to make it a home by the river. All the character and outfit patterns are replicated and reduced to be the perfect dollhouse dimensions. The **1:12 Dollhouse Scale** section discusses how to tackle the miniaturized mammals shown here. Fancy going even smaller? There are tips for that, too!

With all that information at your fingertips, you can feel confident as you select the characters and accessories you want to make. Read through the instructions first, gather your tools and materials, transfer the patterns, and settle down to a relaxing and rewarding crafting session. Time will slow down as you ramble through the pages—let your imagination wander with Ratty and his friends as you stitch new adventures into life.

Introduction

Meet Otter!

Although Otter does not have a starring role in *The Wind in the Willows*, I could not leave him out completely! The chapter "The Piper at the Gates of Dawn" features Otter and his young son Portly, and is a favorite for so many readers.

You can find an additional downloadable pattern for Otter on Bookmarked Hub: **www.bookmarkedhub.com**.

With Otter's instructions and the 1:12 scale adaptations in this book, you can create Otter and Portly to fill out your cast of characters.

Before You Begin

Although the animals are small, they take time and patience. If you are short of time, why not break up the process? Cut everything out one evening, assemble the body the next, then the head, and so on. Within a week, you will have a completed critter to enjoy and share. As you become more familiar with the construction process, it will take less time. But before you embark on your first character, reading this section will help you achieve the best results, and have relaxing, fun crafting sessions!

Essential reading

Tools & Materials: This section covers most of the tools and materials included in this book, including the Basic Sewing Kit and materials more specific to creating each individual character.

Basic Techniques: Here you will find all you need to know about the techniques used in this book. This section includes a complete stitch guide, instructions on making starting and ending knots, hiding knots, strong felt seams, how to hold your work, and much more!

Resources: This section includes a helpful list of where to find the tools, materials and other supplies used in the book.

You Will Need lists

Before you begin any project in this book, read its **You Will Need** list to ensure you have all the tools and materials to hand. These include the **Basic Sewing Kit** detailed in **Tools & Materials**, and a list of specific requirements for the particular project (such as felt, thread, and other fun materials) described in **Creative Materials**.

Seam allowance

All the patterns in this book have their seam allowance of 1.5mm (approx. 1/16in) included.

It is small, but works perfectly with 100% wool or wool-blend felt at this scale. Use it for synthetic and bamboo felt too, but reduce the stuffing density so that the seams are not compromised.

Felt: right & wrong sides

Felt has no right or wrong side, but to achieve a beautiful finish, we stitch some seams on the outside (right side) and others on the inside (wrong side). *Gray shading* is used to indicate the *wrong side of the felt* throughout this book.

Transferring the patterns

1. First, copy and print the patterns using a home scanner and printer. Remember to copy them at 100%—all the patterns in the book are printed to scale, and include their seam allowances.

2. Carefully cut out all the paper pattern pieces—accurate cutting will ensure that the felt pieces fit easily together—and refer to the **Pattern Layout** diagram to ensure the most efficient fabric consumption. Felt is non-woven, so there is no need to follow a grain line.

3. I don't recommend pinning the paper pieces to the felt as that distorts small pattern pieces. Instead, depending on the technique you are using, attach the templates to the felt as follows:

Taping paper patterns: Attach small rolls of washi tape to the back of the pattern pieces, then adhere them to the felt.

Basting (tacking) paper patterns: Thread a needle with a single strand of floss and make a Basting Stitch (see **Basic Techniques**) around the perimeter of each pattern piece to temporarily hold the paper to the felt.

Iron-on freezer paper: Cut out and arrange the freezer paper pieces on the felt with the plastic (shiny) side down. Pass a dry iron (set to high) over the freezer-paper pieces, bonding them to the felt. This takes just a second or two. Carefully cut out the felt around the pattern pieces (see **Basic Techniques**), then peel off the freezer paper. Freezer paper pieces can be reused several times, so don't throw them away! If the felt fibers lift with the freezer paper, simply give the felt another quick press to smooth its surface.

4. Once the pattern pieces are arranged and attached to the corresponding felt colors, rough-cut the felt to separate them, then carefully cut out each individual piece of felt. Cut only one layer of felt at a time, as cutting multiple layers will distort small pieces. Cutting single layers ensures accuracy with small pieces.

Cutting thread

The length of stranded floss (embroidery thread) you stitch with can either make stitching pleasurable or do quite the opposite! Roughly 50cm (20in) is perfect for small projects like this. It is better to change thread more often than experience the tangling and breakage that happens with a lengthy piece.

To get the perfect floss length every time, unwind, refold and cut your skeins into eight 1m (39in) lengths. For general stitching, cut 1m (39in) pieces in half. If a longer piece is needed, use the full length. I cut off the color number from the skein label and slip it onto the flosses for reference. To store the cut floss, I fold each bundle into a loose slip knot and store them together on binder rings.

Face painting on felt

Once you have gathered the materials needed to make your first character, I recommend testing your paint and brushes, or pens, on spare scraps of the felt you are using. Test both with and without the dried hairspray-stiffened surface so you know how they will behave before moving on to paint the final creation (for more information see **Tools & Materials**). I've used slightly different techniques for each animal, so refer to the animal chapters for specific details.

Tools & Materials

In this section you will find details of the Basic Sewing Kit used for all of the projects in the book. This includes basic sewing and craft tools, and items you may already have at home. The Creative Materials section lists the felt, stranded floss (thread), paint, notions, and other colorful, fun materials that bring your characters to life! Turn to the Resources section for guidance on finding everything you need, including details of some my personal favorites used in the book.

Basic sewing kit

For cutting felt

This trio of tools makes cutting felt easy and accurate.

Rotary cutter

In combination with a non-slip, clear acrylic ruler and self-healing cutting mat, rotary cutters are ideal for making perfectly straight cuts in felt. A 45mm blade is ideal for these small-scale projects.

Self-healing cutting mat

Self-healing cutting mats come in various sizes, with both metric and imperial measurements. A small one will do for the projects in this book.

Clear, non-slip acrylic ruler

Acrylic rulers facilitate accurate positioning with a clear view through to your work and the gridded cutting mat below.

Stuffing tools

For stuffing, you will need a basic bamboo skewer or a stuffing fork.

Bamboo skewer

These are available in most grocery stores and make a perfect stuffing tool; the slight roughness to their blunt end is ideal for pushing stuffing into narrow places.

Stuffing fork

A stuffing fork (see **Resources**) is a fantastic upgrade to a skewer, with a two-pronged end that easily grabs fiber and helps direct it exactly where you want it.

Needles

Embroidery needles

Although you can sew with virtually any needle, I recommend embroidery needles (combined with stranded embroidery floss/thread) for my designs. By choosing the smallest size that you can happily thread, your needles will pass through the felt smoothly for more enjoyable stitching. I recommend choosing a size between 8 and 10 (10 being the smallest).

Long darners

We use long needles designed for darning for attaching eyes. Sizes 5 or 7 are the perfect length and diameter to pass through the shaft of sew-in eyes.

Pins & clips

I like short, glass-headed straight pins, and 25mm (1in) long is the perfect length for small projects. A fantastic alternative are wonder clips—as soon as I tried them, we became inseparable!

Marking tools

You will need a few marking tools. For tail, snap, and button placement, use a pencil or water-soluble marking pen. For marking straight lines, a tailor's chalk-wheel is ideal.

Scissors & wire cutters

Choose a small pair of scissors, 15cm (6in) in size, for cutting paper patterns, felt, and channels for stuffing. I prefer spring-loaded, easy-grip scissors without finger holes. A pair of craft scissors is useful to cut chipboard, and wire snips are ideal for cutting through pipe-cleaners and the wire used for Mole's glasses.

Rulers

I recommend having two types of rulers at hand. A 15cm (6in) ruler is a handy size to use while constructing your animals. Use it to measure symmetrical arm lengths, to check small measurements, and for buttons and pocket placement. A small, clear, non-slip acrylic ruler is also a handy tool (see **Basic Sewing Kit**). This ruler is a must-have to accurately cut the Luncheon Basket in the **Accessories** section.

Fast-drying tacky glue

Two versions of tacky glue are readily available and equally useful: all-purpose and a thicker, fast-grabbing variety. The thicker variety has a faster dry time and is so thick that it almost holds on by itself (as if 50% of the water was removed from the all-purpose version). Really great stuff! If you decide to make the Wingback Chair (and why wouldn't you?!), a much more aggressive glue is required to glue on rather, than sew on, the legs. Intrigued? All is revealed in that project.

Needle-nosed pliers & tweezers

Needle-nosed pliers are just the thing to turn out tiny sewn heads, turn up mini cuffs, and for dainty buttoning. They are also helpful for grabbing onto and pulling needles in tricky situations. Tweezers double as a finer version of pliers for tasks like picking up beads and buttons, adjusting whiskers, and so on.

Utility knife

I suggest keeping a small breakoff-blade utility knife to hand. Choose one with a locking screw that securely holds the blade in place (see **Resources**). These are excellent because you can always have a new sharp edge with a quick crack of the blade (along its score lines). Use it to cut the chipboard in the Wingback Chair and the stiffened felt in the Luncheon Basket. Even if you don't make those, it is still a useful and versatile tool to have in your kit. Alternatively, use a craft knife with a replaceable blade.

Washi tape

Also known as Japanese masking tape, washi tape's low-tack adhesive is repositionable without pattern tearing. Use it to attach patterns to felt without pinning or basting (tacking). Remove it and store patterns for later use.

Plain paper or freezer paper

Depending on the technique you use to transfer the patterns to the felt, you will need regular plain paper or freezer paper. Refer to **Before You Begin** for more information about transferring patterns, including using freezer paper.

Tailor's wax

When working with embroidery floss (thread) and other threads, tailor's wax can come in handy. Waxed floss prevents tangles and can aid in needle threading.

Non-aerosol hairspray

I use extra-hold hairspray to stiffen felt in preparation for painting. Because I brush it on, I use the non-aerosol variety. Unlike starch and acrylic stiffeners, it leaves no residue and will not melt when an iron is used to smooth the surface after drying. Simply pour a little into a small bowl, and paint it on using a soft fluffy brush. It can also be used (as a spray) to tidy up felt surfaces that have become fluffed from handling.

Iron

A basic domestic iron is an essential tool when sewing. In this book it is used unconventionally, sitting upright on its base. Prepare your animal's head with hairspray and let it dry completely, then heat your iron to high. Hold its handle with one hand and the animal's body in the other, then press the head against the surface of the iron. Rotate and shift the head over the surface until it is smooth all over. Now the head is ready for paint or fineliner pen detailing!

Creative materials

Felt

There are several types of felt available—here are my tips for working with whichever one you choose.

Wool blend felt

My creations are designed and made with a wool/rayon blended felt (1mm thick). For me, this is an ideal material—it is all-natural, strong like 100% wool felt, but has a slightly softer hand and no itchy feel! What's not to like?

Other types of felt

100% wool felt is lovely and works for my designs. Although it comes in a 1mm-thickness like wool-blend felt, it is slightly less pliable at this small scale. This won't affect the making of the animals themselves. But if you find that narrow sleeves, slippers, or pant legs are snug, add a slim margin of additional seam allowance to the problem spots (approx. 1mm). Vegan felts, both synthetic and bamboo, work for all my designs, but are not as strong as 100% wool or wool blend. You may need to reduce the amount of stuffing used inside the heads to account for the weaker seams.

Embroidery floss (thread)

Sold in skeins, each length of floss contains six strands. These can be separated and used individually or in groups depending on the thickness you want.

In this book, one strand is used for most general sewing of animal bodies. Two strands are used to connect necks and tails (for extra strength). On clothing, use one strand for seams and fine border stitching (running stitch on hems and cuffs) or two strands for a bolder stitch that highlights a contrasting color.

Wool stuffing

I only use 100% wool stuffing in all my designs. I prefer natural fibers and, unlike cotton and bamboo, wool has a springy nature that is perfect for filling without creating lumps.

Cotton pipe cleaners

I use 100% cotton pipe cleaners. Made for cleaning smoking pipes, they have a more robust internal wire than the craft-store chenille variety. In addition, the cotton is bulkier, so they double as armature and stuffing for limbs. They are readily available online (sold for crafting) and in smoke shops.

Cotton pipe cleaners generally come in two thicknesses: standard and plush. I use the fuller, plush size to fill arms and legs. The craft-store version can be used, but you may need more (or a pinch of stuffing) to fill out the legs and arms.

Removing the cotton fluff

At times, the projects will ask you to trim some of the cotton fluff from the wire to help fit into narrow spots. To remove the fiber, angle the blade of your scissors parallel to the pipe cleaner, and cut away the fiber down to the wire. Work in rows, turning the pipe cleaner as you go. Don't worry about how it looks—it doesn't need to be beautiful!

Acrylic paint pens

I was over the moon when I discovered acrylic paint pens! They opened up a new world of possibilities for my creature creations; I hope you come to love them as much as I do! There are many brands to choose from (see **Resources** for my favorites).

Many animals have multi-colored faces, and although a lot can be done with sewing and layering felt, paint pens can add a new and exciting dimension!

Nib sizes

There are several different styles of nibs for fine and broad markings. Fine nibs suit my small-scale projects. A 0.7mm nib is perfect for very fine lines (see Ratty's fur markings and the white details on Toad's wingtip shoes). For a slightly broader line, I use a 1mm nib.

How to use

Before each use, shake well, then press the nib down onto a piece of scrap paper until the paint begins to flow from the nib. When using, hold the pen at an angle so that the nib catches less on the felt fibers.

Acrylic paint & paintbrushes

For more variation, I also experimented with regular acrylic paints and brushes on the felt, which I have explained and illustrated so makers of all levels can enjoy the process!

Diluted or undiluted?

For several projects, I recommend using acrylic paints directly from the tube, without water. On hairspray-prepared felt, thick, tube paint makes a smoother, opaque layer than can be achieved with thinned paint (see Badger's face stripes and the black on Toad's wingtips). For applications where a sheer layer is desired, you can thin the paint into a watery wash and make translucent layers of color, as used for Mole's face painting.

Soap trick

When using paint that has been diluted, it can sometimes bead up instead of absorbing into the felt. You can help the paint to sink in by adding a tiny bit of simple grease-cutting dish soap (washing up liquid). The soap will help break the surface tension of the fiber, allowing the paint to be absorbed rather than repelled by the felt. The reason that this is not necessary when using full-strength paint directly from the tube (undiluted) is that this thick paint is meant to sit on the surface.

Brushes

These are the brushes I use and recommend if you are in the market for a few new ones. For cutting sharp edges, use a 6mm or 10mm (¼in or ⅜in) angled shader brush. For fine lines and details, a no. 2, 4, or 6 round brush is suitable. For hairspray application, use a fluffy no. 4 quill brush. With so many shapes and sizes, there will be others that work just as well. If you already have brushes, find the closest and give it a try.

Trial run

No matter which paint and brush you use, test them first on prepared felt scraps so you know what to expect before painting your character.

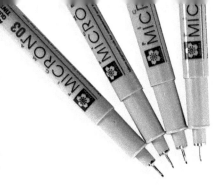

Fineliner pens

I recommend these for adding fine details such as mouths and nostrils. Choose only waterproof, permanent pens, so that if the markings ever come into contact with water (as you work or afterward) the markings do not bleed.

Wire & jump rings

You never know when wire and jump rings will come in handy for miniatures! We use both to make Mole's glasses, but you can also use jump rings for belt hardware (see **Adding Details**). Fine gauge wire is always popping up in my patterns, and I know you will find many uses if you add it to your craft stash!

Sticks & picks

Small pieces of wood can provide endless possibilities for miniature creations! We will use flat toothpicks for a fishing drop line, and coffee stirrers and craft sticks as luncheon-basket weaving tools (see **Accessories**).

Snaps

For our small scale, 5–6mm snaps work well. 6mm snaps are more widely available as they are also used in human-scale dressmaking! They are generally available in several finishes, but antique bronze and gunmetal are my favorites.

Snap finesse

When attaching the two sides of a snap, begin by attaching the nipple side to the underside of the garment's overlapping edge. This side of the snap is slimmer and can more easily be stitched to the underside surface of the felt with no stitching showing on the front (where decorative buttons may be attached). Wait until the garment is completed before attaching the dimple side. Fit the garment to the animal, and press the nipple into the felt of the opposite side of the garment. Lightly mark the indentation with a pencil, then stitch the dimple side of the snap perfectly in place.

Sew-in eyes

We will use 4mm, 5mm, and 6mm sew-in eyes (not safety eyes). I prefer plastic eyes with a short shank on the back to glass eyes with a long looped wire shank. Glass eyes are beautiful (do not hesitate to try them), but the long, looped wire shank is trickier to install for beginners.

Fitting the shank

For the lip of the eye to sit flat on the face, the eye hole (in the head) must be slightly larger than the shank (**fig. 1**) on the back of the eye. Test the eye hole size by setting the shank into it. If the hole is too small, enlarge it with the sharp end of your skewer until the shank drops in easily.

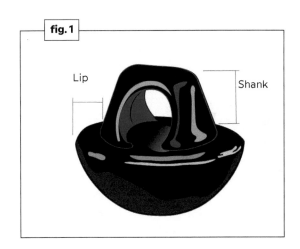

fig. 1

Lip

Shank

Buttons & beads

Miniature buttons are available online in various materials, shapes, and sizes for dollmaking. I have used 4mm (⅛in) buttons in antique bronze and gunmetal throughout the clothing projects. You may like to have 3mm buttons on hand for a size change on cuffs.

An alternative to traditional buttons for our animals is super duo beads. These small two-hole beads come in an endless rainbow of colors and are widely available. You can even use tiny glass seed beads as shining fish eyes (see **Accessories**) or as bright embellishments on miniature outfits.

Basic Body

To create our cast of characters, this is where it all begins! All four animals—Toad, Mole, Ratty, and Badger—share the same basic body construction, with a cleverly designed, built-in, posable armature (frame). Once you get the hang of the basic body, you'll be on your way to filling the Riverbank, Meadow, and Wild Wood with many felt friends!

Choose your patterns

Before you do anything else, see **Patterns: Templates** *to select the correct patterns for your character's body.*

For all animals
See **Basic Techniques** for guidance on whipstitch and blind stitch.

Basic body A
- Ratty
- Badger

These patterns include pieces for the basic torso, arms, and legs of these two characters. Note where to mark the torso with the tail placement. The animals' unique tail construction can be found in their individual chapters.

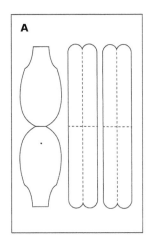

Basic body B
- Mole

These patterns include pieces for the basic torso, arms, and legs of Mole. His limbs are shorter than those of his friends above, and of course there is no need to mark a tail placement.

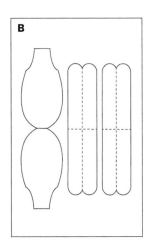

Basic body C
- Toad

These patterns include pieces for the basic torso, arms, and legs for Toad. There is no need to mark a tail. Being an amphibian, he has very different limbs to those of his friends! Their unique assembly instructions and the way they're connected to the armature are included in Toad's chapter.

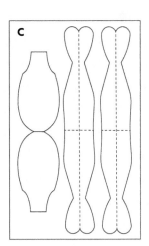

YOU WILL NEED

Felt pieces:*
- 1 torso piece (this piece forms the front and back torso)
- 1 legs piece (this piece makes both legs)
- 1 arms piece (this piece makes both arms)

*See **Before You Begin** *for how to transfer the pattern pieces, referring to the individual animal's chapter for details of colors and quantities. Remember to select the relevant set of patterns as shown, and to mark the tail, eyes, and button placements.*

Other tools and materials:
- 6-stranded embroidery floss (thread) to match the animal
- Embroidery needle, size 8 or the size of your choice
- 5 extra-plush cotton pipe cleaners, 30cm (12in) long, *or* 7 regular craft-store chenille stems (pipe cleaners)
- Pipe cleaner folding template in the correct size (see **Prepare the Pipe Cleaners** Step 1 and **Templates**)
- Wool stuffing, 2g for torso*
- Stuffing tool: bamboo skewer or stuffing fork
- Strong non-aerosol hairspray
- Fluffy paintbrush
- Basic sewing kit

*Wool weight measurements are only a guide. Bellies should be soft and squeezable and heads should be firmly packed (except Toad's—he is soft-headed).

Make the limbs & torso

Prepare the pipe cleaners

1. Cut a pipe cleaner folding template from chipboard (size Large for Ratty and Badger, and size Small for Mole). You may also use the cardboard from a sturdy cereal box or the back of a notebook to make the template (but avoid using thick material like corrugated cardboard).

2. Mark both the center (fold to) lines on the chipboard, as shown on the pattern.

3. The plushness of the folded pipe cleaners will fill out the leg and arm tubes. If you have extra-plush cotton pipe cleaners, use four in total; if you are using standard chenille stems (pipe cleaners), use six. (These illustrations feature the extra-plush type.)

4. Fold the pipe cleaners around the template, trimming their ends (with wire snips or craft scissors) to the marked lines at the template's center. Leave a gap between the cut ends (**fig. 1a**). Remove them from the folding template and separate them into two bundles of two, or two bundles of three, depending on the type of pipe cleaner.

5. Match the folded ends of the first pipe cleaner bundle. Secure the ends with plastic wonder clips, then tightly wrap their center with floss (embroidery thread) to securely bind the cut wire ends (**fig. 1b**). Finish with a square knot (right over left, then left over right) to hold the bundle securely together. Repeat this process on the remaining pipe cleaner pair(s).

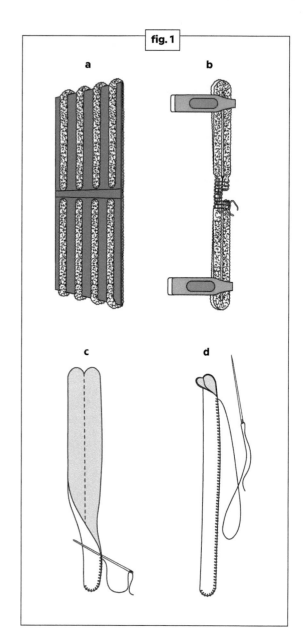

fig. 1

a   b

c   d

Stitch the legs & arms

1. Thread your needle with a single strand of embroidery floss (thread) and make a starting knot at one end. Stitch the side seams of the leg and arm tubes. Work with a length of floss approximately 50cm (20in) at a time.

2. Fold the felt legs tube in half lengthwise, hide the starting knot inside the fold at one end, and begin to whipstitch (see **Basic Techniques**) the tube edges together (**fig. 1c**). Whipstitch along the length of the tube, leaving the opposite end open (**fig. 1d**). Repeat Steps 1–2 for the arms tube.

3. Slide the first pipe-cleaner bundle into the legs tube, then repeat on the arms tube. The pipe cleaners should fit snugly, so you will have to slip them in a short distance at a time to prevent them from buckling. Hold both the tube and pipe cleaner close to the entrance as you work, keeping the wire straight. Once the pipe cleaner is fully encased, stitch the end closed.

Assemble the armature

The twisted pipe cleaner in fig. 2 is shown in white and gray for clarity

1. Fold the leg piece in half at its center point, matching the feet (ends) exactly. Fold the remaining pipe cleaner in half and twist it around the center point of the legs piece to form the spine of the animal (**fig. 2a**).

2. Lay the felt torso piece on a flat surface and position the armature over it. Ease the torso front through the legs with its narrow point at the crotch (**fig. 2b**). Twist the pipe cleaners of the spine (to create the torso section), then insert the arm piece between the spine pipe cleaners, just below the corners of the shoulders and twist again to hold the arms in place (**fig. 2c**).

3. Trim the pipe-cleaner spine to 2.5cm (1in) above the neckline (**fig. 2d**).

Binding the pipe cleaners prevents their sharp cut ends from catching on the felt as they slide into the leg and arm tubes in Step 3.

If the pipe cleaner seems too long for its tube, the felt may have compressed as you inserted it. To lengthen the tube, grasp it at either end in clasped fists and tug outward. This action will stretch the length of the felt tube, reversing any compression.

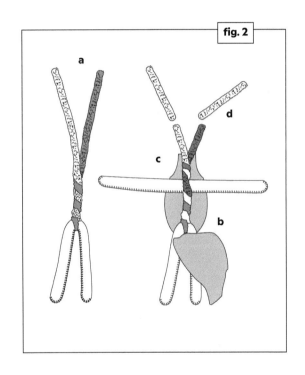

fig. 2

Stitch the torso & hip seams

1. As before, thread your needle with a single strand of floss (thread) and make a starting knot at one end.

2. Bring the front of the torso piece up over the front of the armature and pin together the back and front at the shoulders (**fig. 3a**). Under one arm, hide your starting knot between the front and back sides of the torso felt. Whipstitch the side seam of the torso from under the arm to the hip (**fig. 3b**).

3. When you reach the hip, transition to an edge-to-surface whipstitch to secure the limbs (see **Basic Techniques**). Bend the opposite leg out of the way (**fig. 3c**) and stitch around the top of the leg, catching the edge of the torso and the surface of the leg with each stitch. When you have been all around and return to the hip, make an ending knot and hide it (see **Basic Techniques**).

4. Repeat on the opposite side of the body, starting again under the arm and working down and around the leg.

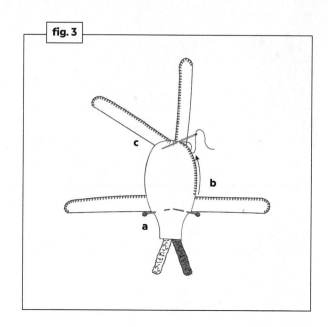

fig. 3

It's fun to give the animals paw prints at the ends of their arms and legs. Use a black or sepia waterproof fineliner pen, size 002 (0.3mm), to mark them onto the felt. A bit of hair spray brushed onto the paw (which is then dried and ironed smooth) will create a smooth surface for the pen. It can be done without stiffening the surface first, but I recommend testing the pen on a scrap piece of felt to get the hang of marking untreated felt.

Stitch & stuff the body

Stuff the lower torso

1. To keep the pipe-cleaner spine centered, stuff the front, back, and sides of the lower torso (**fig. 4a**). Using a pinch of stuffing at a time and your stuffing tool (see **Tools & Materials**), fill the cavity up to the arms without over-packing the stuffing, or later on the clothing may be too snug.

Upper torso seams

1. As before, thread your needle with a single strand of floss (thread) and make a starting knot at one end.

2. Begin at the top of the neck on the first side (**fig. 4b**), hiding the knot between the front and back of the torso felt. Whipstitch from the neck to the shoulder corner, then knot off at the shoulder and hide the knot. Repeat on the opposite side. Do not stitch around the arms until you've stuffed the upper body.

Stuff the upper body

1. After stitching both sides of the neck (but not around the arms), use your stuffing tool to begin filling the upper body with stuffing. As you work, bend the neck's exposed pipe cleaners out of the way. Avoid overfilling the chest where the arms cross the spine. A barrel chest may cause some of the clothes to be snug.

2. Fill the neck up to the opening (retaining its slimness) and avoid overstuffing (which can stretch the felt out of shape).

Stitch around the arms

1. Slide the arms from side to side as needed to center them in the torso. Each arm should measure about 6.5cm (2½in) from the torso to its rounded end.

2. Secure the arms to the body (**fig. 4c**) with an edge-to-surface whipstitch as you did with the legs (bending them at the shoulder as necessary).

3. Fold over the ends of the pipe cleaner at the neck (**fig. 4d**). Later, this allows them to slide up into the head without snagging. As an optional step, I sometimes tightly bind the two pipe cleaners together with floss after folding them down. Wrapping them supports the wire for head attachment. If you decide to try it, use the pipe-cleaner binding technique (see **Prepare the Pipe Cleaners**, Step 5).

> Stitching around the legs (and later, the arms) may seem awkward when you start, but my hybrid whipstitches are a great way to gracefully get out of tricky spots. See **Basic Techniques** to learn about whipstitch and its variations.

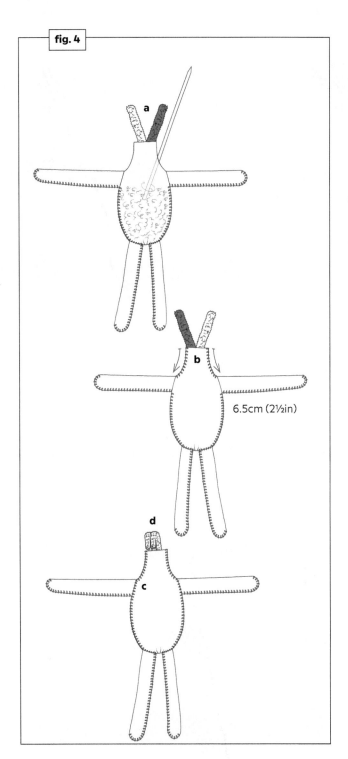

fig. 4

6.5cm (2½in)

Stuff the head

Preparing the head

To prepare your animal's head for for stuffing, first choose the relevant head pattern pieces (see **Patterns**) and turn to your character's chapter for step-by-step stitching instructions. Then you'll be ready to come back here!

The instructions here show Ratty, but Mole and Badger share the same attachment method. Special instructions for Toad can be found in his individual chapter.

Choose your tool

Insert small quantities of wool fiber, one little bit at a time, into the head using one of two stuffing tools:

- **Using a bamboo skewer:** Use the blunt end of the skewer and twist it as you push fiber into the cavity. The slightly rough end "grabs" hold of the fiber as you direct it into place **(fig. 5)**.

- **Using a stuffing fork:** This tool is very accurate! The two-pronged end holds the fiber as you push and direct it into place.

Go slowly and gently with whichever tool you choose, remembering to add only small amounts of stuffing at a time for the best results.

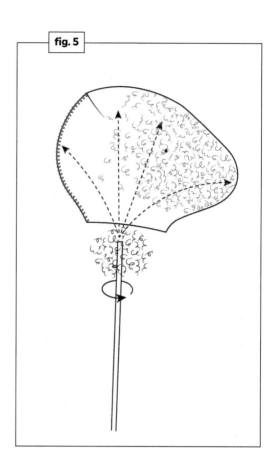

fig. 5

Tips & Techniques

HOW FIRM?

It is surprising how much stuffing you can pack into a small space. For heads, tightly packing the filling stretches out the seams and adds fullness and dimension. It also provides a smooth, flat surface for adding facial markings (with ink and paint), and a firm core when you come to stitch and indent the eyes. (However, as you have learned in **Stitch & Stuff the Body**, the animals' bodies should feel more like a marshmallow. Too much fullness will affect the fit of the clothing.)

SCISSOR CHANNEL TECHNIQUE

- When the head starts to feel full, but it's difficult to find more space, cut a channel through the stuffing with the sharp point of your scissors. This will create a space for you to insert more stuffing into the center core of the head.

- If there is a soft spot at the surface, snip and tunnel up to the spot and slide stuffing through the channel to fill it out.

- This same channel technique is also used when attaching the head to the body to create a hole for the pipe cleaner.

TARGETED STUFFING

- Targeted stuffing can be added in two ways, with either the scissor channel technique or by sliding stuffing between the core of wool and the felt's surface.

- Think of this process as sculpting from the inside out. Once the head appears nearly full, add stuffing to targeted areas to subtly increase their volume.

- Targeted stuffing refines the head shape—for example, adding more fiber to the cheeks to plump them or adding volume to the back of the head if it is not symmetrical.

Attach & prepare the head

To create your chosen animal's head, first turn to its specific chapter for step-by-step instructions, then come back here. The following illustrations feature Badger's head (fig. 6) and Ratty's head (fig. 7), but Mole's head shares the same attachment and preparation methods.

Attaching the head

1. With a sharp pair of scissors, snip up into the head, through the stuffing, to make a generous pathway for the neck pipe cleaners (**fig. 6a**).

2. Insert the neck pipe cleaners up into the channel you just cut. Push the head and body together so that the head overlaps the neck by approximately 7mm (¼in) (**fig. 6b**).

3. Thread your needle again, this time with *two* strands of floss (thread) and make a starting knot at one end.

4. Use blind stitch (see **Basic Techniques**) to attach the head to the body. Stitch twice around the neck for strength. Finish with an ending knot, hiding it beneath the felt surface (see **Basic Techniques**).

Disguising the seams

1. Use a pin to scratch the surface along the length of the center seam and darts to gently lift a halo of felt fibers (**fig. 7a**). This is the start of a great-looking combover!

2. Turn *off* the steam setting of your iron, and set the temperature to "high". With the iron resting securely on its stand, carefully press the seam and darts against the plate to flatten the lifted fibers (watch your fingers!). Like magic, the visible stitches are hidden beneath the flattened crossing fibers (**fig. 7b**).

This is transformative for everyone, but beginners will love the process of hiding rogue stitches as they perfect their technique!

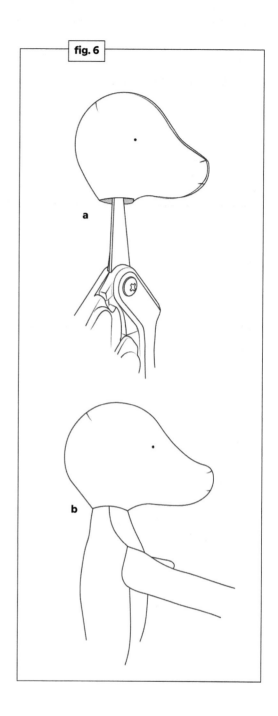

fig. 6

Making the eye holes

1. Use the sharp end of the skewer to make holes at the eye markings (**fig. 7c**). These will accommodate the shaft of the eye that we add later.

Stiffening the surface

1. Cover your work surface to protect it from hairspray drips.

2. To prepare the surface of the head for face paint, you will apply hairspray. Begin by pouring extra-firm hold, non-aerosol hairspray into a small dish (**fig. 7d**).

3. Using a fluffy paint brush, brush the hairspray over almost the entire surface of the head. Just avoid a small margin around the neck so that the seam will remain flexible for positioning and posing (**fig. 7e**).

4. Allow the head to dry completely (this can take several hours to overnight). Then flatten its surface with a hot iron as before (bend the head as necessary to reach around the contours). Once it is evenly smooth all over and hard to the touch, the head is ready for painting (**fig. 7f**).

fig. 7

a

b

c

d

e

f

Basic Body

Make an extra head to practice your stitches, stitch tension, and stuffing. Pack it tightly to test the strength of your stitches. Are they all holding? Is the tension even? Can you firmly fill the head without stitches pulling through the felt edge? Practice stuffing so that the head proportions are even and not lopsided. What can you do to make it better on the real thing? After some practice, you'll truly be able to make any of the animals from head to toe!

25

Basic Jacket

You will find the patterns for all the clothes in the **Patterns** section, and cutting instructions in **Before You Begin**. Just like each animal's personality, each jacket varies in its style and cut, resulting in a set of outfits designed and sewn specially for each character.

However, the basic construction of their jackets remains the same, with one combined piece for the front/back (main body) and two sleeves. For their specific detailing, see each individual character's chapter. The coat used in this example of the basic assembly is Ratty's nautical-inspired navy peacoat.

EXTRA FEATURES

Each animal's jacket has its own special details, which not only look impressive, but are also fun to stitch!

- **Mole's blazer:** see his chapter for Edge Stitching, Buttonhole, and Back Collar

- **Ratty's peacoat:** see his chapter for Edge Stitching, Snap Fastening, Belt, and Buttons

- **Badger's dressing gown:** see his chapter for Painted Pattern, Edge Stitching, and Back Belt

- **Toad's tailcoat:** see his chapter for Edge Stitching, Embroidery, Pockets, and Center-Back Coat Tail

Any of the animals' garments can be modified to fit their friends! Here are a couple of sartorial suggestions:

To alter Toad's coat for animals with tails, omit the center back panel of the tailcoat.

To alter Badger's dressing gown for animals without tails, cut the back slit, as usual, omitting the tail hole and the contrasting belt below the tail.

Mole's clothes fit his taller friends beautifully. His blazer makes a wonderful short-sleeved top and his pants become shorts or swim trunks!

Useful terms

SETTING IN SLEEVES

This is the process of attaching the curved shoulder of the sleeve into the armhole of the main body of the jacket.

TAB CUFFS

These wrap around the wrist end of the sleeve. A decorative button, bead, or cross-stitch holds them down to the wrist opening of the sleeve. On the pattern, they protrude at a right angle from the sleeve's narrower, flat (wrist) end.

UPTURNED CUFFS

These are simply cuffs folded up.

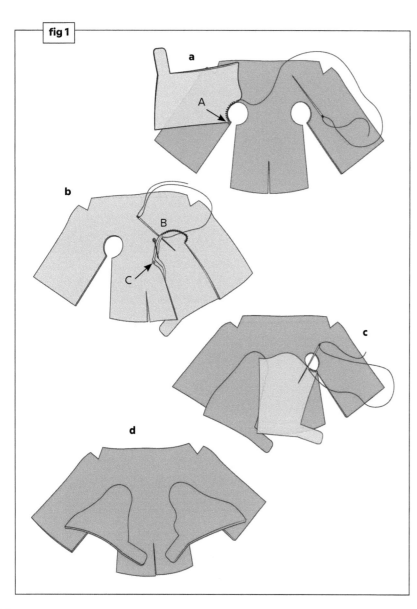

fig 1

Making the basic jacket

Turn to each animal's individual chapter where you will find listed all the tools, materials, and instructions needed for their extra features. Although felt does not have a right or a wrong side, some seams are stitched on the inside of the jacket and others are stitched on the outside. In these illustrations, gray indicates the inside of the jacket.

Setting in sleeves

1. Thread your needle with a single strand of embroidery floss (thread) to match the color of the jacket, and make a starting knot at one end.

2. Match the corners of the shoulder and armhole at point A (**fig. 1a**). (For tab cuff sleeves, attach them in the orientation shown throughout **fig. 1**.)

3. Whipstitch a few stitches of the seam, then pivot the shoulder edge to match the curve of the armhole and make a few more stitches. Continue this way until the center point of the shoulder and armhole meet at point B.

4. Match and pin the opposite corners at point **C** to hold them in place as you finish whipstitching the shoulder seam (**fig. 1b**).

5. When you reach the corner at point C, knot off on the wrong side and repeat on the remaining shoulder seam (**fig. 1c**). The jacket now has both sleeves set into the shoulders (**fig. 1d**).

For jackets with upturned cuffs or without cuffs, disregard the tabs in these illustrations and refer to the details of the particular jacket you are making.

6. After the side and sleeve seams are eventually complete, the tabs will wrap around the wrist hole. Tab sleeves can be set into the jacket in the opposite orientation as long as they're symmetrical to make a left and a right sleeve. If you accidentally set them in with two rights or two lefts, cut off the tabs—no one will be any the wiser!

Side seams and sleeve seams

1. Match the lower side-seam corners (**A**) and Whipstitch up the side seam to the armhole (**B**) (**fig. 2a**).

2. If your floss (thread) is long enough, pass the needle through the armhole (**fig. 2b**) and continue Whipstitching the sleeve seam on the right side of the jacket. If your floss (thread) is too short, knot off and begin again as usual (under the arm) on the jacket's right side.

3. Whipstitch the sleeve seam from the juncture under the arm up to the tab (**fig. 2c**) if you have one.

Cuffs and sleeve patches

Tab cuffs

Wrap them around each sleeve and attach with a cross-stitch (**fig. 3a**). Use the wrist hole as access, hiding your starting knot inside the sleeve. Alternatively, if you're stitching buttons to the tabs, make your stitching through the button's holes.

Upturned cuffs

Both Mole's blazer and Badger's dressing gown have up-turned cuffs. On a flat pattern, upturned cuffs appear with a flare at the end of the sleeve and a dashed fold line. The extra fabric of the flare allows the cuff to fold over the sleeve without it puckering (**fig. 3b**). For sleeves with upturned cuffs, stitch from the armholes down the sleeves to the wrist (**fig. 3c, A to B**) and knot off on the right side of the fabric. To fold up the cuffs you'll need a pair of needle-nosed pliers, or nimble fingers, and a bit of patience to make the turn. Your ending knot will be hidden when the cuff is folded up.

Elbow patches

To give any of the animals' jackets extra detail, add a pair of elbow patches (**fig. 3d**), cut from a contrasting color of fabric for a bold look or a harmonizing color for an understated effect. Attach with an edge-to-surface whipstitch before assembling the jacket.

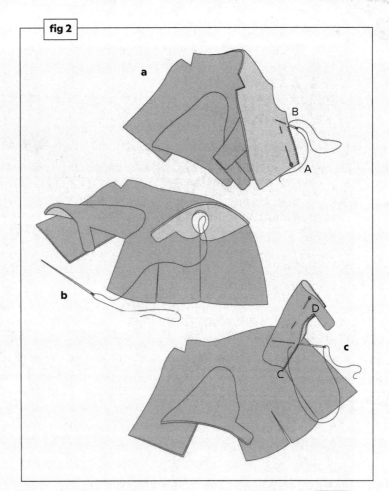

fig 2

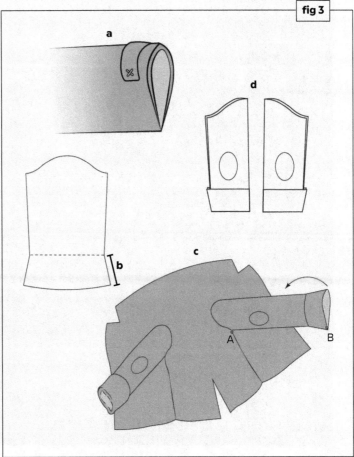

fig 3

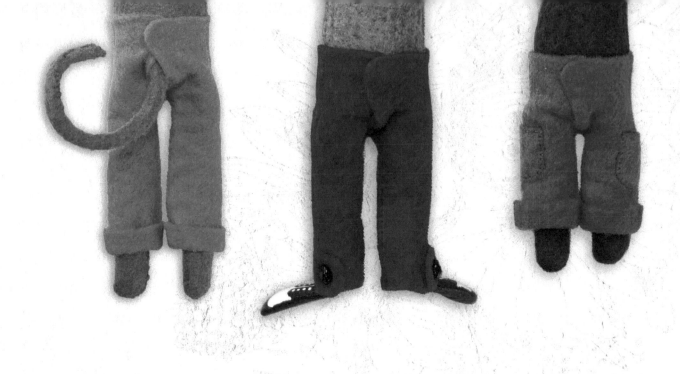

Basic Pants

You will find the patterns for all the clothes in the **Patterns** section, and cutting instructions in **Before You Begin**. Each animal wears a different outfit to suit their day-to-day adventures, and even their pants are designed and sewn specially for them.

Fortunately, the basic pant construction remains the same for all, with a front and a back pattern piece. Each style has a back-snap closure fitting animals both with and without tails, so garments can be shared between them. For their specific detailing, see each individual character's chapter for instructions. In the meantime, Ratty's golden pants are used here to illustrate the basic assembly process.

EXTRA FEATURES

- **Mole's side-pocket pants:** see his chapter for Attaching Pockets

- **Ratty's cuffed sailor pants:** see this section for instructions (there are no extra features)

- **Toad's slim-cut tab-cuff pants:** see his chapter for Tab Cuff Detailing

Note: There is no pants pattern for Badger, as he is wrapped in a cozy full-length dressing gown.

Useful terms

INSEAM

An inseam is the inner seam of the pants (connecting the front to the back between the legs). It runs from the ankle, up the leg to the crotch, and down to the opposite ankle.

TAB CUFFS

These wrap around the ankle edge of the pant leg on Toad's pants. A decorative button, bead, or cross-stitch holds them down to the ankle opening of the leg. On the pattern, they come out at a right angle from the ankle end of the pant leg. If you don't want tab cuffs on a garment with them, cut them off by folding each leg lengthwise and matching the inseam and side seam. Cut off the tab at the same angle as the opposite side of the leg.

UPTURNED CUFFS

These are simply cuffs that fold up, giving structure to the ankles.

Making the basic pants

Turn to each animal's individual chapter where you will find listed all the tools, materials, and instructions needed for any extra features.

Snap (nipple side)

1. Thread your needle with a single strand of embroidery floss (thread) to match the color of the pants, and make a starting knot at one end.

2. Using the marking on the back pattern piece as a guide, place and sew on the nipple side of the snap (**fig. 1a**) (see **Tools & Materials** for more instructions).

3. With the nipple side of the snap attached, this becomes the *wrong side* of the back pants piece.

Wait to attach the remaining dimple side of the snap until the pants are complete so that they can be fitted to the animal you're making.

Side seams

1. Thread your needle with a single strand of matching embroidery floss (thread), and make a starting knot at one end.

2. Lay the front and back pant pieces together, with right sides facing. Baste (tack), pin, or use wonder clips along the side seams to stop them from shifting as you stitch. Whipstitch from the hip down to the fold line at the cuff (**fig. 1b**).

3. Open and fold back the sides of the leg and continue whipstitching on the opposite side to the end of the seam. Knot off on the same side (**fig. 1c**).

4. Repeat on the opposite leg.

Inseams

1. Turn the pants right side out, thread your needle with a single strand of matching floss, and make a starting knot at one end.

2. Whipstitch from the bottom corner of the inseam (**A**) around the crotch (**B**) then back down to the bottom corner of the opposite leg (**C**) (**fig. 2a**). As you stitch the inseam of each leg, it helps to pin the leg you are not working on out of the way (**fig. 2b**).

Cuffs & snaps (dimple side)

1. Turn up the cuffs of the pants using a pair of needle-nosed pliers (or nimble fingers!) (**fig. 2c**).

2. Fit the pants on your animal, crossing over the back tail flap. When you have a good fit, press the nipple side of the snap into the felt below to make an indentation.

3. Mark the indentation (optional) and remove the pants.

4. Center the dimple side of the snap over the indentation and/or mark (**fig. 2d**) and stitch it onto the felt (see **Tools & Materials** for more instructions).

For invisible stitching, when cuffs are turned up, switch the side you stitch on (on the side seams) at the cuff fold. It is not necessary to do this on the inseam because that stitching is already on the outside.

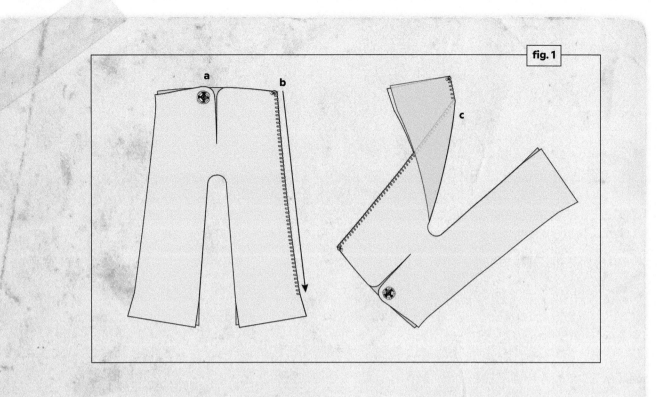

fig. 1

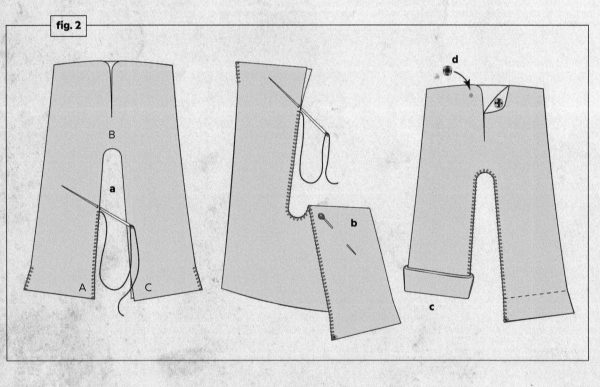

fig. 2

Adding Details

They say "it's all in the details", and with everything we have covered, you have what you need to go far beyond where Kenneth Grahame or I have taken you! Our animals need not be the only friends on the River Bank, Meadow, or the Wild Wood. Why not change body colors to make male and female animals to create families? Expand the fun and invent new stories! The clothing, too, can be styled in new ways to build a more comprehensive wardrobe. Here are a few ideas to get you started.

Make a short-sleeved shirt from Mole's blazer

Omit the collar band on the back of the neck, add a breast pocket, and trim the edge with a buttonhole stitch. Now you have a short-sleeved shirt for mole's taller friends. Shorten the sleeves by half to make one for mole.

Belts

Another classic detail is a belt, which looks great on any vest (waistcoat) or jacket. Cut different shapes and sizes to complement the garment. Adding a jump ring to each end of a half back-belt is also very dapper!

Transforming a dressing gown

Both the overall length and sleeves of Badger's dressing gown can be shortened for Mole, and I believe that this is just the beginning! I can imagine this robe with a slimmer closing edge and collar, made in camel-colored felt, as a driving trench for Toad. It could be significantly shortened in length and sleeves to create a smoking jacket. But why stop at men's attire? Add an asymmetrical button and embroidered flowers to create a beautiful 1920s-style winter coat! A touch of narrow velvet ribbon would trim the front and collar nicely.

Earrings, patches, & pockets

In the story "Wayfarers All", Ratty meets a dusty, weary, traveling rat with a gold earring and patched pants. To add a hoop earring (or two) to your animals, use a simple jump ring (found in the bead or jewelry-making section of craft stores). Bend it open slightly, place over the edge of the ear, and squeeze closed. You can even make a small hole in the ear with a punch or the sharp end of a skewer to thread the wire through. Before clothing assembly, use edge-to-surface whipstitch to add small square patches in various sizes to the knees and seat of the pants. You can also add elbow patches and patch-pockets to jackets using the same technique. Try different sizes and shapes, stitch detailing, and colors!

Fabric patterns

Polka dot: this works for any garment, not just Toad's slim pants. The great thing about polka-dot patterns is that they are universally snappy on all genders! If you are making an animal for a child, choose colors they love. Kenneth Grahame's characters may have all been male, but you're free as a bird to create the gender that suits you!

Plaid: plaids are fun to create with fine-nib paint pens! Add your favorite pattern to decorate clothing, chairs, and blankets. Vests (waistcoats) are a simple garment to start with because you don't have to match the pattern along any seams. If the garment is made of two or more pattern pieces, draw the plaid on the cut felt pieces before assembly.

1:12 Dollhouse Scale

I originally designed my animals at a size to suit children's little hands, but more and more adults are making them both for themselves and as gifts. People often ask how tall the animals are and if they fit in a 1:12 scale dollhouse. The answer is yes, sort of. The full-scale animals in this book (and in my line of kits) finish at about 16cm (6¼in) tall. This makes them just over 1.8m (6ft) tall in a 1:12 scale environment.

The 1:12 scale measurement is based on the imperial measuring system, where 1in equals 1ft.

Inside the dollhouse

The full-size animals are broader than traditional dollhouse inhabitants, so need more space between furniture to navigate rooms without knocking things about. You'll find that some furniture will be too petite, while other pieces are generous in size and so fit them just right. Some furniture pictured in this book is 1:12 scale, while others were made especially for the sets.

Making 1:12 scale patterns

Because dollhouse collectors and enthusiasts may want to size the animals down, I have supplied a second set of animal and outfit patterns scaled down to 80%. An 80% scale puts them at a more universal dollhouse size, making Ratty and Badger approx. 13cm (5¼in) and a much better height and width to live comfortably in a tiny house. Toad finishes slightly shorter, and Mole is more child-sized at 80%.

Smaller still...

You can go even smaller—in the past I have made the animals at 70% and 60%. As you reduce their size, they become perfect Christmas ornaments! If you do scale the animals to 60% or less, you may want to sew on the clothing, as closures can become a challenge.

Reducing patterns

Use the scan/copy function on your home printer to reduce the patterns to the size of your choice. Alternatively, take them to a local copy center or print shop, and they will help you. If the staff are concerned about copyright laws, I've included a little note with permission to copy on the last page of the book.

Making smaller animals

Construction doesn't change much when you reduce the size of the animals, but they will work up a bit more quickly with less stitching! Here are some tips for basic adjustments:

FELT THICKNESS

As the animals reduce in size, the felt thickness appears more significant. Reducing felt thickness is unnecessary for smaller animal bodies, but it will make their clothes fit much better. For wool-blend felt, use a hot iron and steam to compress the felt—I can reduce the felt's thickness by almost half doing this!

SEAM ALLOWANCE & DARTS

Maintain the usual seam allowance on 80%, 70%, and 60% reduction. However, the darts get smaller as the patterns shrink, so take your time and make careful stitches, reducing the space between them.

PIPE CLEANERS FOR ARMS & LEGS

At 80%, reduce the pipe cleaner quantity to one plush folded pipe-cleaner inside the leg and arm tubes. The cotton fluff of one folded pipe cleaner will not completely fill the tubes at 80%, but that is ok. If this bothers you, rather than filling them more, I recommend narrowing the tubes slightly for a snug pipe cleaner (and better clothing) fit.

If you reduce the patterns further (to make child-sized dollhouse characters or ornaments), simply fill the legs and arms tubes with a quantity of pipe-cleaner that fits the tubes best. When using a single thickness of pipe-cleaners for the smallest animals, trim the cotton fluff from their cut ends so that you can fold the sharp wires over. If plush pipe cleaners are too thick, use regular thickness or the craft-store chenille variety.

TOAD'S ARMS & LEGS

Toad's arms and legs assemble nicely at 80% scale. Trim, curve, and bind the first pipe cleaner, as shown in Toad's chapter (Legs & Arms, step 3), reducing its length to fit the scaled leg piece. Keep the loop binding below the narrow ankle so that only one trimmed thickness of pipe cleaner passes through the ankle. Bind only one short pipe cleaner to the center portion of the leg (rather than the three graduated pieces used at full scale).

The Animals

Now it is time for you to meet the animals themselves! Everything you require is detailed in the **You Will Need** lists, including colorful materials such as felt, thread, and paint. I have marked clearly wherever you need to refer to another section of the book. It's time for you to bring Mole, Ratty, Badger, and Toad to life—happy stitching!

"What, Ratty, my dear little man!" exclaimed the Badger, in quite a different voice. "Come along in, both of you, at once. Why, you must be perished. Well I never! Lost in the snow! And in the Wild Wood, too, and at this time of night! But come in with you."

The rapid nightfall of mid-December had quite
beset the little village as they approached it on
soft feet over a first thin fall of powdery snow.
Little was visible but squares of a dusky orange-
red on either side of the street, where the firelight
or lamplight of each cottage overflowed through
the casements into the dark world without.

The Mole struck a match, and by
its light the Rat saw that they were
standing in an open space, neatly
swept and sanded underfoot, and
directly facing them was Mole's
little front door, with "Mole End"
painted, in Gothic lettering,
over the bell-pull at the side.

Mole

Who among us has not caught the fresh, keen scent of spring and been inspired to clean? Deep within his burrow, Mole feels that innate sensation. It emanates from the air above and the lowly soil of his home below, and thus it begins. After cleaning and whitewashing—transferring much of the dust and dirt to his fur—it all becomes too much! Kenneth Graham perfectly captures the spirit of that need to be outdoors and breathe in the bright, green scents of spring; to feel new life burgeoning around us after a long winter. In the book, Mole pops up from the earth wearing a black smoking jacket, but I imagine him in something a bit more colorful so I've designed a pea-green blazer, carrot-orange pants, and a garnet-colored cap. An outfit sartorially appropriate for his meadow, river, and woodland adventures ahead, which he enjoys more than spring cleaning...

He suddenly flung down his brush on the floor, said "Bother!" and "O blow!" and also "Hang Spring cleaning!" and bolted out of the house without even waiting to put on his coat. Something up above was calling him imperiously and he made for the steep little tunnel... "Up we go! Up we go!" till at last, pop! his snout came out into the sunlight, and he found himself rolling in the warm grass of a great meadow. "This is fine!" he said to himself. "This is better than whitewashing!"

Making Mole

MOLE'S PATTERNS

For the pattern pieces for Mole's body, head, blazer, and pants, see **Patterns**.

MOLE'S BODY & HEAD CONSTRUCTION

To construct Mole's limbs and torso see **Basic Body**. Mole's unique head can be found in this chapter. For information on making strong seams and stuffing see **Basic Techniques**.

MATERIALS

The **You Will Need** list includes a combination of items from both the **Basic Sewing Kit** and **Creative Materials**. Refer to **Tools & Materials** to learn about everything listed.

YOU WILL NEED

FOR MOLE'S HEAD & BODY

- Charcoal-colored felt, 17 x 21cm (6¾ x 8¼in)

- 6-stranded embroidery floss (thread) in a color to match the felt

- 5 extra-plush cotton pipe cleaners, 30cm (12in) long, *or* 7 regular craft-store chenille stems (pipe cleaners)

- Pipe cleaner folding template, size small (see **Basic Body** and **Patterns**)

- Wool stuffing, 7–8g (5–6g for the head and 2g for the torso)*

- 2 sew-in eyes, 4mm (approx. ⅛in)

- Fine-grit sandpaper or an emery board (optional)

- Acrylic paint, pale pink (or a mix of darker pink/red and titanium white acrylic paint)

- 3 small mixing dishes and one jar of water (for paint)

- No. 6 round watercolor paint brush

- Waterproof fineliner pen, black, size 005 (0.2mm)

- Basic sewing kit (see **Tools & Materials**)

*Wool weight measurements are only a guide. Mole's belly should be soft and squeezable and his head firmly packed.

Gray shading is used to indicate the wrong side of the felt throughout the illustrations (see **Before You Begin**).

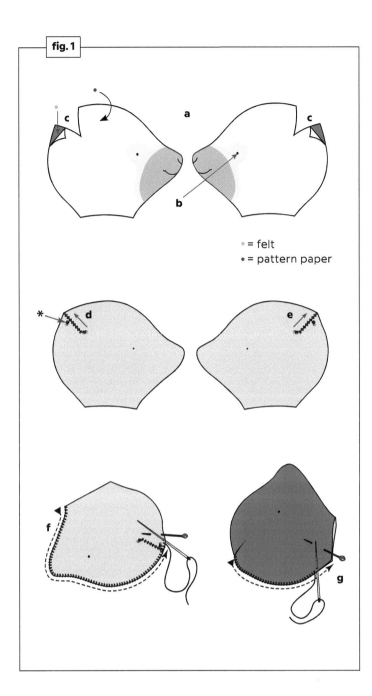

fig. 1

• = felt
• = pattern paper

Body

Make a body (see **Basic Body** and **Patterns**) in charcoal felt (or another felt color of your choice) before assembling the head.

Head

MARK THE EYE PLACEMENT

1. With the paper pattern pieces still attached to the felt, lay the side-head pieces nose to nose on your work surface (**fig. 1a**). Note the placement of the blue and red dots.

2. Thread a needle with one strand of embroidery floss (thread) in any color—this marking stitch will be removed—and make a starting knot at one end. Stitch from front-to-back through the black dot of each eye (**fig. 1b**). Knot the thread on the wrong side. Remove the paper pattern, popping the knot through the paper as you do so.

STITCH THE TOP HEAD DARTS

The V-shaped cuts in the side-head pieces are called darts (**fig. 1c**). (See **Basic Techniques**).

1. Thread a needle with one strand of matching floss (thread) and make a starting knot at one end.

2. Pinch the first dart, matching the sides of the V-shape. Whipstitch from the base of the V to the top edge (**fig. 1d**). Repeat on the opposite side of the head (**fig. 1e**).

STITCH THE CENTER SEAM

1. Thread a needle with one strand of matching floss (thread) and make a starting knot at one end.

2. Match the two side-head pieces with right sides together, and use a pin or wonder clip to hold the aligned darts in place (**fig. 1f**). Whipstitch the seam following the dashed line and knot off a few stitches beyond the dart.

3. Carefully turn the head right side out. Use the blunt end of a bamboo skewer or a pair of needle-nosed pliers to assist in turning. Whipstitch the back of the head closed leaving the neck hole open (**fig. 1g**).

Avoid catching your needle on the ending knots (✱) when you stitch the center seam (**fig. 1f**) by setting them back from the edge of the felt (see **Basic Techniques**).

Mole

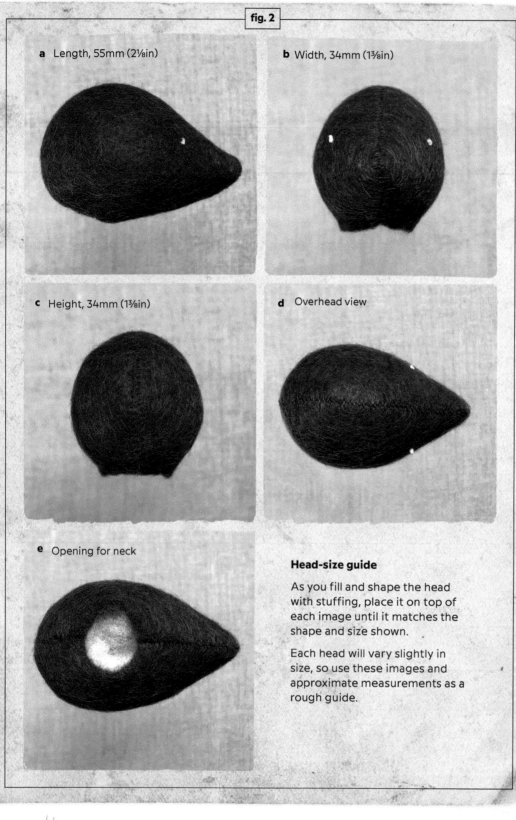

fig. 2

a Length, 55mm (2⅛in)

b Width, 34mm (1⅜in)

c Height, 34mm (1⅜in)

d Overhead view

e Opening for neck

Head-size guide

As you fill and shape the head with stuffing, place it on top of each image until it matches the shape and size shown.

Each head will vary slightly in size, so use these images and approximate measurements as a rough guide.

FINISH THE HEAD

To create the head, see **Basic Body**, which tells you how to:

- Stuff the head (see **fig. 2** In this chapter for Mole's dimensions)
- Attach the head
- Disguise the seams
- Prepare the surface

Face

Before preparing its surface for painting the face, attach the head to the body (see **Basic Body**). See **Tools & Materials** to learn more about the different options for face painting.

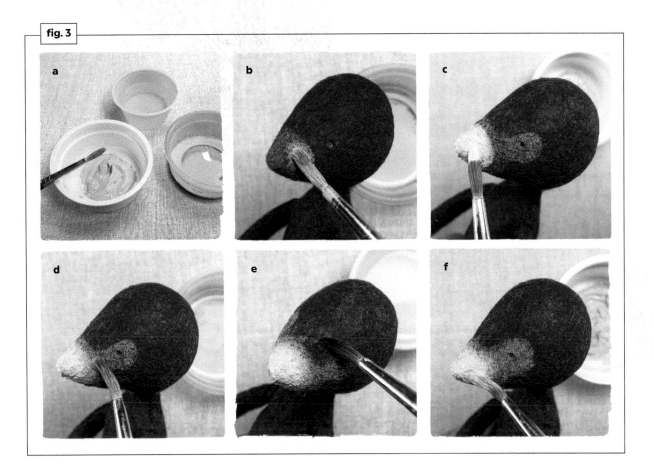

fig. 3

a b c d e f

Mole

PAINT THE FEATURES

1. Into the first of your three mixing dishes, add the pink paint with **no** water. In the second dish, add a small amount of water, then add a little pink paint, using the brush to make a watery wash of pink liquid. Fill the third dish halfway with clean water (**fig. 3a**).

2. Use the clean brush and the watery pink wash to paint around the pointed snout in an even circle (**fig. 3b**).

This watery wash layer will eventually dry to a sheer shadow of color. I use this method to map out the area for the subsequent layers of paint.

3. Continuing with the pink wash, paint a semi-circle around each eye hole, then clean and dry the brush. While the first layer around the snout is still wet, use the thick paint to add a shorter opaque pink circle to the end (**fig. 3c**). Clean and dry the brush.

4. Use the pink wash to blend the edge of the thick paint into the surface of the thinner wash of paint (**fig. 3d**).

5. Clean the brush, then use the clean water in the third dish to blend the watery pink wash into the gray felt beyond the snout (**fig. 3e**). Let the paint dry completely before moving on.

6. When the paint is completely dry, lightly sand the nose with fine-grit sandpaper or an emery board (optional). When you later mark the nose and mouth, it will be easier to do so on a smoother surface. After sanding, add a final coat of paint around nose (**fig. 3f**). Wipe the brush bristles of excess paint and "dry brush" a soft coating of paint around the eye holes to deepen their color as necessary.

Although not essential after every step, cleaning and drying the brush between actions gives you more control of your paint application.

45

ATTACH THE EYES

1. Thread a long darning needle with two strands of embroidery floss (thread) and make an ending knot. Pass the needle through the head from right to left to lodge the knot in the interior stuffing (**fig. 4a**).

2. Pass the needle back through to the opposite side to fully secure the knot in the head (**fig. 4b**).

3. Thread the needle through the shaft of the first sew-in eye, then pass the needle through the head from right to left (**fig. 4c**).

4. Add the second eye, then pass the needle through to the opposite side (**fig. 4d**). Repeat, catching each eye shaft one more time.

5. Pull the floss (thread) taut to indent the eyes, then knot off the thread (**fig. 4e**). Insert the needle under the eye (exiting anywhere) and pull through to pop the knot below the eye.

6. Use a black waterproof fineliner pen to draw on the nose and mouth as shown (**fig. 4f**).

If you decide Mole's mouth or nose need adjustments, simply allow the pen markings to dry, then paint over them. When the paint has dried, you can give it another go.

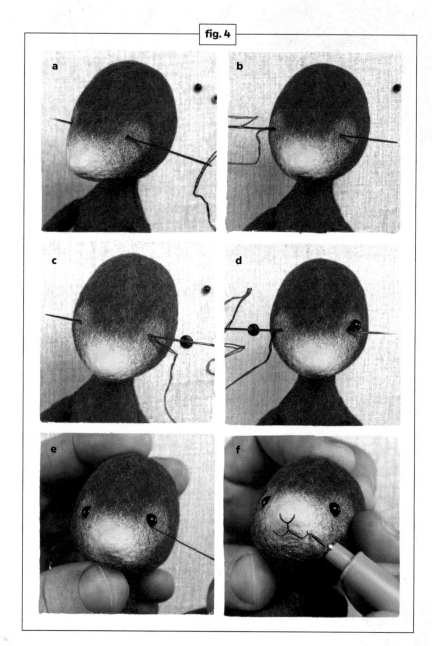

fig. 4

Mole

46

Mole's Outfit

A colorful ensemble, perfect for Mole's springtime adventures.

MOLE'S PATTERNS

For the pattern pieces for Mole's blazer, pants, and cap, see **Patterns**.

MOLE'S BLAZER

Read through the instructions here first, then see **Basic Jacket**. Much of the detailing described in this section (buttons, back collar, and topstitching) can be completed before you embark on assembling the jacket itself.

MOLE'S PANTS

See **Basic Pants** for the foundation of the design, and refer to this section to add the special side-seam pockets.

YOU WILL NEED

FOR MOLE'S OUTFIT

- Pea-green felt (blazer), 15 x 15cm (6 x 6in)
- Carrot-orange felt (pants), 14 x 9cm (5½ x 3½in)
- Teal felt (pant pockets and collar band), 5 x 4cm (2 x 1½in)
- Garnet felt (cap), 14 x 9cm (5½ x 3½in)
- Pumpkin felt (cap band) 5 x 2cm (2 x ¾in)
- 6-stranded embroidery floss (thread), 1 skein each in pea-green, carrot-orange, teal, garnet, and copper tones to match and complement the felt colors
- 1 button, antique bronze, 4mm (approx. ⅛in)
- 2 two-hole glass seed beads, teal, 2.5 x 5mm (approx. 1/16 x ¼in) or tiny buttons
- 1 snap, antique bronze, 6mm (approx. ¼in)
- Basic sewing kit (see **Tools & Materials**)
- Chipboard, 0.75mm thick, or 540gsm card stock

FOR MOLE'S GLASSES

- 26-gauge wire, bronze, 35cm (14in)
- 2 18-gauge jump rings, antique bronze, 8mm diameter

See **Tools & Materials** for more information about everything in Mole's **You Will Need** list.

TO PREPARE

Cut the pattern pieces for Mole's clothes from the felt and chipboard (see **Patterns**). You will find patterns for his blazer, pants, and cap.

Blazer

On the pea-green felt pieces, complete the detailing (edge trim, button, and buttonhole, and back-collar gathering and collar band) as follows. Then for the main construction of the blazer, see **Basic Jacket**.

EDGE TRIM

For the bold, colorful border, use two strands of teal floss (thread). Make a single row of running stitch (see **Basic Techniques**) around the outer edge of the blazer, and a double row on the cuffs (see the teal dashed lines in **fig. 5**). Make all starting and ending knots on the wrong side of the blazer.

BUTTON & BUTTONHOLE

Stitch the button to the blazer using the pattern as a reference for placement (**fig. 5a**). Use buttonhole stitch (see **Basic Techniques**) to finish the inside edge of the buttonhole (optional).

BACK-COLLAR GATHERING & COLLAR BAND

Thread a needle with two strands of a matching-color floss (thread). Use running stitch to gather the felt between the two points below the collar. This will draw in the center back collar and make it stand up smartly. Center and pin the contrasting collar band over the gathering. Use an edge-to-surface whipstitch (see **Basic Techniques**) to attach the band (**fig. 5b**).

Mole's clothes fit everyone! On taller animals, his pants become shorts or swim trunks. The blazer (minus the back-collar band) makes a wonderful short-sleeved top!

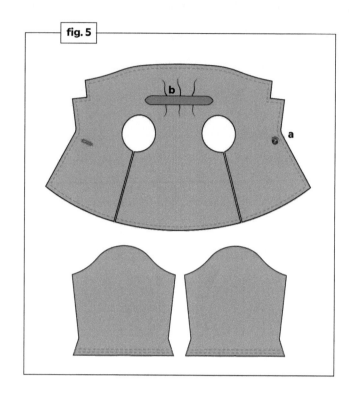

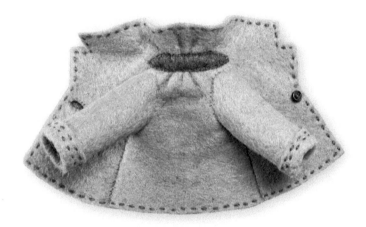

Pants

Stitch the side seams of the pants (see **Basic Pants**, figs 1a, b, and c), then turn the pants "tube" right side out. Before stitching the inseam, attach the side-seam pockets with an edge-to-surface whipstitch. For easier access to each side seam, fold the pants "tube" at the center front and back, then pin the opposite leg to the waist to get it out of the way as you stitch each pocket (**fig. 6**). After attaching the pockets, continue sewing the inseam as directed in the **Basic Pants** chapter.

Glasses

1. Cut a 35cm (14in) length of 26-gauge wire and mark its center point with a small piece of tape, then partially open the two jump rings. Positioning the first jump ring about 1 cm (⅜in) to the right of the tape, begin wrapping the wire around around it. Wrap the wire around the jump ring forming a tight coil around half of the ring. Repeat the process, wrapping the second ring, leaving approx. 15mm (½in) for the bridge of the glasses (**fig. 7a**).

2. Close both jump rings, then trim the arms of the glasses to about 5cm (2in) long. Wrap the cut ends of the wire around the end of a bamboo skewer to make a coil at each arm end (**fig. 7b**).

3. Position the glasses on Mole's face and pin them to the sides of his head. Attach the coiled ends by stitching back and forth through Mole's head, catching the coils on either side (**fig. 7c**). Avoid pulling so tightly that an indent is created by the stitches. When the glasses are secure, knot off the thread and insert the needle once more (exiting anywhere) and pull through to pop the knot beneath the felt surface.

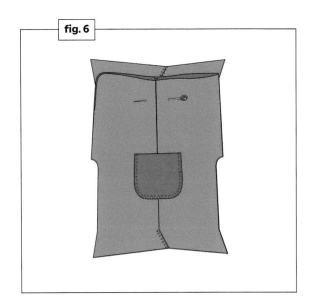

fig. 6

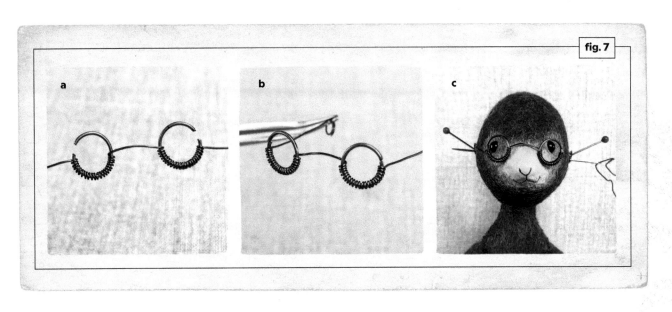

fig. 7

a

b

c

49

Cap

1. Thread a needle with two strands of matching floss (thread) and make a starting knot at one end. Make a tightly spaced running stitch around the circumference of the cap's top circle, 1–2mm (approx. 1/16in) from its edge. Turn your iron to its high setting.

2. Center the chipboard circle on the felt circle, then draw in the floss (thread) to tightly gather it around the chipboard. With the floss (thread) held taut, use the iron to press and steam the felt until the gathers are flattened and the felt has a crisp edge around the chipboard (**fig. 8a**).

3. Gently open the gathered edge (without detaching the floss/thread) and remove the chipboard disc. Draw the floss (thread) in and press again to hold the shape.

4. Remove the needle, leaving the stitching gathered and the tail attached. Thread the needle with two strands of contrasting copper-colored thread (floss) and make a starting knot at one end. Stitch around the outer edge using buttonhole stitch (see **Basic Techniques**) (**fig. 8b**). When complete, knot off on the inside of the cap.

5. Lay the rectangular brim felt with the cut hole over the gathered side of the felt disc. Gently expand the gathered edge to fit the hole, maintaining uniform gathering all the way around (**fig. 8c**).

6. Pin the gathered edge to the cut edge. Thread a needle with a single strand of matching floss and make a starting knot at one end. Whipstitch (see **Basic Techniques**) around the edge (**fig. 8d**). When you've come full circle, knot off and trim off the floss (thread) used to gather the edge.

7. To cut the brim shape from the pattern rectangle, start by securing the paper pattern to the underside of the cap, matching the holes (**fig. 8e**). Use double-sided tape or small rolls of washi tape to help keep it in place. Cut away the felt around the pattern piece to achieve the final shape of the brim.

8. Finish the cap with running stitch around the outer edge of the brim, then attach the front band with two-hole seed beads (super duo beads) or buttons at either end (**fig. 8f**).

Finishing the crisply pressed crown edge with a contrasting buttonhole stitch holds the fold and makes a handsome detail on Mole's cap.

Mole

fig. 8

Ratty

Oh, how I love Ratty and his easy way with friends and poetry, boats, and picnics! He's a generous and kind soul, and the best of friends to Mole, Badger, and Toad. Being a Water Rat and a mariner at heart, it seems only right that Ratty should have a peacoat with golden pants and a crimson cravat to match the colors in the Royal Marine's flag! Ratty's peacoat features a faux double-breasted placket (with snap closure), a half-back belt, tab-cuff sleeves, and contrasting edge stitching. With the coat so handsomely detailed, I kept the pants and cravat simple. But you can still mix things up by adding pockets, embroidery, edge stitching, or whatever details you like. It just depends on your time, imagination, and the materials at hand. See the **Adding Details** section for more ideas to get creative and make your own uniquely styled Ratty!

*"Nice? It's the only thing," said the Water Rat solemnly, as he leaned forward for his stroke. "Believe me, my young friend, there is **nothing**—absolutely nothing— half so much worth doing as simply messing about in boats. Simply messing," he went on dreamily: "messing—about—in—boats; messing—"*

Making Ratty

RATTY'S PATTERNS

For the pattern pieces for Ratty's body, head, ears, and tail, see **Patterns**.

RATTY'S BODY & HEAD CONSTRUCTION

To construct Ratty's limbs and torso, see **Basic Body**. Ratty's unique head and tail construction can be found in this chapter. For information on making strong seams and stuffing, see **Basic Techniques**.

MATERIALS

The **You Will Need** list includes a combination of items from both the **Basic Sewing Kit** and **Creative Materials**. Refer to **Tools & Materials** to learn about everything listed.

YOU WILL NEED

FOR RATTY'S HEAD & BODY

- Camel-colored felt, 17 x 21cm (7¾ x 8¼in) (or another felt color of your choice)

- 6-stranded embroidery floss (thread) to match the felt, 16.5 x 20cm (6½ in x 8in)

- 6 extra-plush cotton pipe cleaners, 30cm (12in) long, *or* 7 regular craft-store chenille stems (pipe cleaners)

- Pipe cleaner folding template, size large (see **Basic Body** and **Patterns**)

- Wool stuffing, 7–8g (5–6g for the head and 2g for the torso)*

- 2 sew-in eyes, 5mm (approx. ³⁄₁₆in)

- Waterproof fineliner pens: black, size 005 (0.2mm)—optional; sepia, size 005 (0.2mm)

- Acrylic paint pen, beige, 0.7mm (or a fine brush and beige acrylic paint and a drop of dish soap/washing-up liquid)

- Basic sewing kit (see **Tools & Materials**)

*Wool weight measurements are only a guide. Ratty's belly should be soft and squeezable and his head firmly packed.

Gray shading is used to indicate the wrong side of the felt throughout the illustrations (see **Before You Begin**).

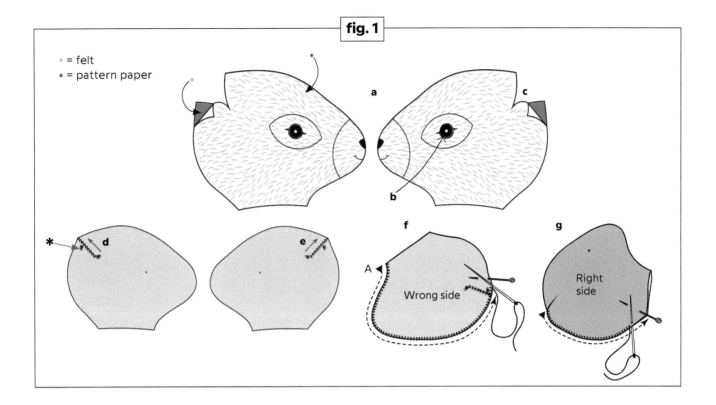

fig. 1

= felt
= pattern paper

a
c
b
* d
e
f
A
Wrong side
g
Right side

Body

Make a body (see **Basic Body**) in camel-colored felt (or another felt color of your choice) before assembling the head.

Head

MARK THE EYE PLACEMENT

1. With the paper pattern pieces still attached to the felt, lay the side-head pieces nose to nose on your work surface (**fig. 1a**).

2. Thread a needle with one strand of embroidery floss (thread) in any color—this marking stitch will be removed—and make a starting knot at one end. Stitch front to back through the white dot in the center of each eye (**fig. 1b**). Knot the thread on the wrong side. Remove the paper pattern, popping the knot through the paper as you do so.

STITCH THE TOP HEAD DARTS

The V-shaped cuts in the side-head pieces are called darts (**fig. 1c**). (See **Basic Techniques**).

1. Thread a needle with one strand of matching floss (thread) and make a starting knot at one end.

2. Pinch the first dart, matching the sides of the V-shape. Whipstitch from the base of the V to the top edge (**fig. 1d**). Repeat on the opposite side of the head (**fig. 1e**).

STITCH THE CENTER SEAM

1. Thread a needle with one strand of matching floss (thread) and make a starting knot at one end.

2. Match the two side head pieces with right sides together, and use a pin or wonder clip to hold the aligned darts in place (**fig. 1f**). Whipstitch the seam following the dashed line and knot off a few stitches beyond the dart.

3. Carefully turn the head right-side out. Use the blunt end of a bamboo skewer or a pair of needle-nosed pliers to assist in turning. Whipstitch the back of the head closed along the seam, following the dashed line; leave the neck hole open (**fig. 1g**).

Avoid catching your needle on the ending knots (✱) when you stitch the center seam (**fig. 1f**) by setting them back from the edge of the felt (see **Basic Techniques**).

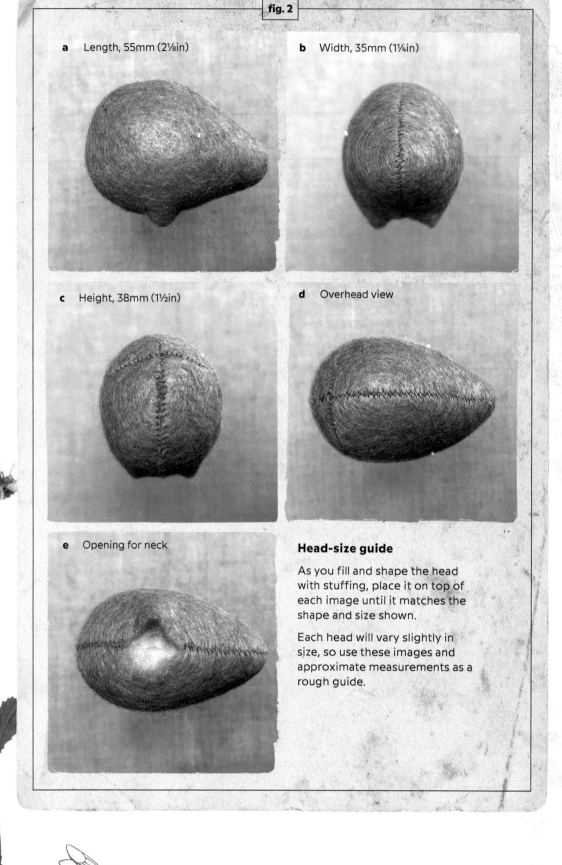

fig. 2

a Length, 55mm (2⅛in)

b Width, 35mm (1¼in)

c Height, 38mm (1½in)

d Overhead view

e Opening for neck

Head-size guide

As you fill and shape the head with stuffing, place it on top of each image until it matches the shape and size shown.

Each head will vary slightly in size, so use these images and approximate measurements as a rough guide.

Ratty

FINISH THE HEAD

To create the head, see **Basic Body**, which tells you how to:

- Stuff the head
- Attach the head
- Disguise the seams
- Prepare the surface

Face

Before preparing its surface for painting the face, attach the head to the body (see **Basic Body**). Refer to **Tools & Materials** to learn more about the different options for face painting.

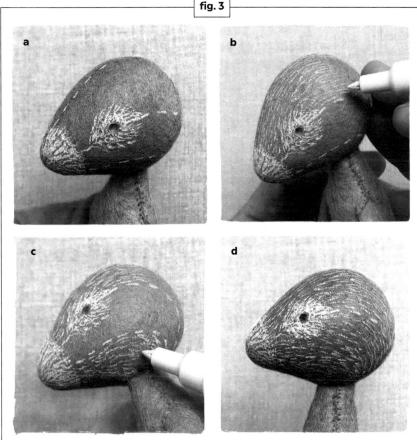

fig. 3

PAINT THE FUR MARKINGS

1. For Ratty's face, use a 0.7mm acrylic paint pen in beige. This color and extra-fine nib size creates fur markings on the camel felt. Always read the instructions for your paint pen and test it on a scrap of felt first (see **Before You Begin**).

2. Prime the paint pen. Hold the nib at an angle (approximately 45 degrees) as you move it lightly over the prepared felt surface to make fine, dashed fur markings.

3. Fill in the dense markings of Ratty's muzzle and eye-patch areas with short pen or brush strokes (see **Before You Begin**).

Then, to guide the rest of the fur markings, make five rows of dashed fur lines—one along the center seam, one passing through each eye patch, and one through each cheek. Continue the lines toward the back of the head, curving down with its shape and ending at the neckline (**fig. 3a**).

4. Fill in the hair between the dashed guidelines more sparsely than you did with the eye patch or muzzle (**fig. 3b**).

5. Fill under the cheek guideline following its shape and the curve of the seam (**fig. 3c**). Fill in the entire head in this manner (**fig. 3d**).

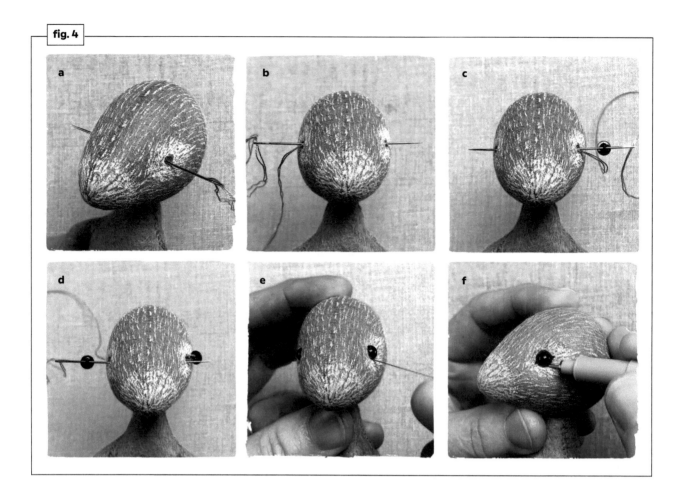

fig. 4

ATTACH THE EYES

1. Thread a long darning needle with two strands of floss (thread) and make a knot in one end. Pass the needle through the head from right to left to lodge the knot in the interior stuffing (**fig. 4a**).

2. Pass the needle back through to the opposite side to fully secure the knot in the head (**fig. 4b**).

3. Thread the needle through the shaft of the first sew-in eye, then pass the needle through the head from right to left (**fig. 4c**).

4. Add the second eye, then pass the needle through to the opposite side (**fig. 4d**). Repeat, catching each eye shaft one more time.

5. Pull the floss (thread) taut to indent the eyes, then knot off (**fig. 4e**). Insert the needle under the eye (exiting anywhere) and pull through to pop the knot under the eye.

6. (Optional) Use a black waterproof fineliner pen to outline each eye (**fig. 4f**). As this size of nib is delicate, use a light touch. Angle the nib at 45 degrees and sneak the tiny nib right up to the edge of the eye as you go; no felt color should remain between the outline and the eye itself. To finish, make a small dash at the front and back of the eye (following the direction of the fur) to create an almond shape.

Ratty can be made with and without face paint. For the unpainted face, use the fineliner pens for the eyeliner and mouth as before (**fig. 4f**), but embroider the nose with a satin stitch (see **Basic Techniques**).

PAINT THE NOSE AND MOUTH

1. Use an extra-fine sepia waterproof fineliner pen, size 005 (0.2mm), to outline the nose (**fig. 5a**). Then fill in with either a larger nib fineliner pen, size 05 (0.45mm), or a matching sepia paint pen, size 0.7mm.

2. Use an extra-fine sepia waterproof fineliner pen to mark in the mouth (**fig. 5b**).

ATTACH THE EARS

1. Pin the top corner of the first ear in place (**fig. 6a**). Then, flip the bottom corner backward and pin it in place (**fig. 6b**). Repeat this step on the opposite side and make sure that the ears are symmetrical.

2. Remove the bottom pin and use a toothpick to apply a small triangle of tacky glue to the bottom corner of the ear (**fig 6c**). Flip the glued surface back, adhering the glue to the head, and pin in place.

3. Remove the top pin and flip the ear back to access the underside of the top corner. Apply the tacky glue as before, then flip the ear forward to adhere the glued corner to the head (**fig. 6d**).

4. Allow the glue to dry, then remove the pins. If there are visible pinholes, gently scratch over them with a pin to disguise them with fiber.

5. Use a paintbrush to apply hairspray to the ears with a fluffy brush, saturating them with the liquid. Then scrunch them with your fingers to give a rippled/wrinkled look to their edges (**fig. 6e**). Allow the ears to dry completely (**fig. 6f**).

> Achieving symmetrical, balanced ears takes patience! Look at the head from the front, top, back, and sides to check their position from all angles. If you decide to move them, cover the old pin marks by scratching them as before. When designing, I move the ears around until I land on the animal's cutest look. Try this yourself—I'm sure the sweet spot will reveal itself!

fig. 5

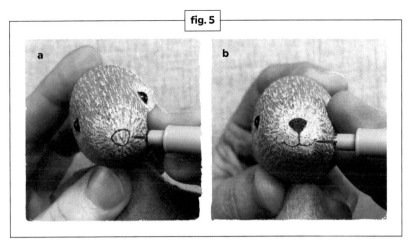

fig. 6

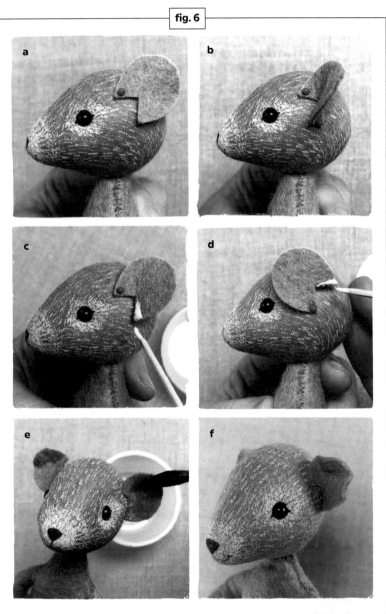

MAKE & ATTACH THE TAIL

1. Cut a length of pipe cleaner approx. 13.5cm (5¼in) long. A single length of either plush or chenille stem will work.

2. Prepare the pipe cleaner as follows: use scissors to remove the cotton fluff from the top 4cm (1½in), trimming the fiber down to the wire. Repeat on the other end, this time removing the fluff only 2.5cm (1in) of the way along.

3. Fold each end over by 1cm (⅜in) to allow the pipe cleaner to slide into the body and tail tube (**fig. 7a**). (If you are using a standard chenille-stem, trimming may not be necessary if it fits into the tail when folded in Step 2).

4. Thread a needle with one strand of floss (thread) to match the tail, and knot one end. Fold the tail felt in half lengthwise along the dashed pattern line. Hide the starting knot between the fold at the base of the tail, then whipstitch (see **Basic Techniques**) up the side (**fig. 7b**), leaving the end open.

5. Insert the trimmed pipe cleaner into the open end of the tail tube, leaving the 4cm (1½in) trimmed end exposed.

6. Make a channel for the tail's pipe cleaner by poking a hole (with the sharp end of a bamboo skewer) up to where the arms cross (**fig. 7c**).

7. Insert the exposed pipe cleaner up into the torso channel. Thread your needle with two strands of floss (thread) and use blind stitch (see **Basic Techniques**) to attach the tail to the body. As you stitch, bend the tail as needed to gain access to the seam (**fig. 7d**).

To remove the fiber from the wire, angle the blade of your scissors parallel to the pipe cleaner and cut away the fiber down to the wire. Work in rows, turning the pipe cleaner as you go. Don't worry about how it looks—it doesn't need to be beautiful!

Ratty

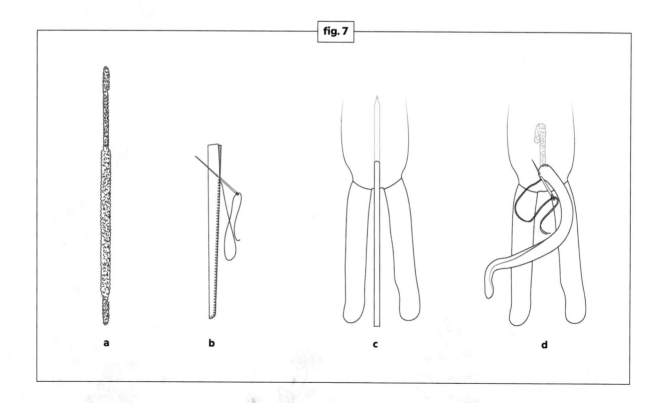

fig. 7

a   b   c   d

60

Ratty's Outfit

In his full outfit, Ratty looks like a gentleman mariner from head to toe!

RATTY'S PATTERNS

For the pattern pieces for Ratty's peacoat, pants, and cravat, see **Patterns**.

RATTY'S PEACOAT

Read through the instructions here first, then see **Basic Jacket**. Most of the detailing (buttons, belt, topstitching, and the first side of the snap) can be completed before you embark on the jacket itself.

RATTY'S PANTS

See **Basic Pants** for the foundation from which all the styles in the book are created. However luckily for Ratty, his pants are used as the example, so go straight there for all the instructions.

YOU WILL NEED

FOR RATTY'S OUTFIT

- Navy felt (peacoat), 16 x 18cm (6½ x 7in)
- Gold felt (pants), 15 x 10cm (5¾ x 4in)
- Red felt (cravat), 13 x 24.5cm (5 x 9½in)
- 6-stranded embroidery floss (thread), 1 skein each in navy, white, and gold to match the felt colors
- 10 buttons, gunmetal (shown) or antique bronze, 4mm (approx. ⅛in)
- 2 metal snap closures, antique bronze, 6mm (approx. ¼in)
- Basic sewing kit (see **Tools & Materials**)

See **Tools & Materials** for more information about everything in Ratty's **You Will Need** list.

TO PREPARE

Cut the pattern pieces for Ratty's clothes from the felt (see **Patterns**). You will find patterns for his pants, peacoat, and smart cravat.

Does your outfit look too crisp and new? If you want your animal's clothes to look lived in rather than just-back-from-the-cleaner perfect, spritz them with water and scrunch them up a bit, then reform to look slightly worn.

Pants

See **Basic Pants**, where the construction of Ratty's pants is shown step by step.

Peacoat

On the navy felt pieces, complete the detailing (buttons, belt, topstitching, and the first side of the snap) as follows. Then for the main construction of the coat, see **Basic Jacket**.

EDGE TRIM

Make a running stitch around the outer edge of the coat. Use a single strand of floss (thread) for a delicate, refined stitch, or two strands for bolder color. Make all starting and ending knots on the wrong side of the coat (see gold dashed lines, **fig. 8**).

BUTTONS

Stitch buttons to the front placket (see buttons, **fig. 8)**, both ends of the belt, and to the tabs of his sleeve cuffs.

SNAP FASTENING

Stitch the snap (nipple side) to the inside of the jacket (see **Before You Begin** for more instructions). Center it between the top four buttons on the front of the jacket (**fig 8a**).

BELT

Attach the belt with a button at each end (**fig. 8b**). If you don't plan to add buttons, make a decorative cross stitch instead.

Cravat

Gently pull the red cravat felt lengthwise with your fingers in small sections. This will have the effect of narrowing it while fluffing up the felt surface and edges so that it doesn't look so freshly cut. Wrap it twice around the neck and tie once.

fig. 8

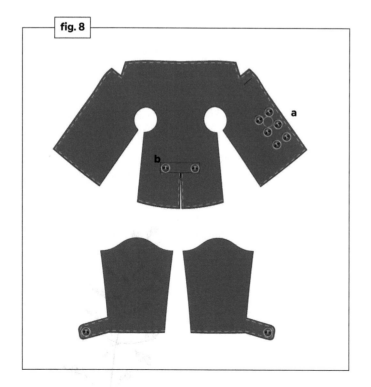

Badger

Always calm, wise, and nurturing, Badger is a great protector of his small friends. On snowy nights deep in the Wild Wood, Badger welcomes travelers into hearth and home for a hot meal and some rest. His underground burrow is peace and tranquility itself—quiet, secure, and snug. "Once well underground, you know exactly where you are," he says, and he has the wisdom to know that he has no control over what happens up above, so he doesn't worry about it. Although he does venture above ground from time to time, Badger believes that peace and security exist only underground. It's where he is at home, so I've chosen warm colors and nature-inspired embellishment for his cozy apparel. Lost in the Wild Wood on a snowy night, Ratty and Mole are fortunate to (literally) stumble across Badger's home. Ringing the doorbell with great relief, the friends are greeted to the sight of him in his very finest night-time attire...

The Badger, who wore a long dressing-gown, and whose slippers were indeed very down at heel, carried a flat candlestick in his paw and had probably been on his way to bed when their summons sounded. He looked kindly down on them and patted both their heads. "This is not the sort of night for small animals to be out," he said paternally. "I'm afraid you've been up to some of your pranks again, Ratty. But come along; come into the kitchen. There's a first-rate fire there, and supper and everything."

Making Badger

BADGER'S PATTERNS

For the pattern pieces for Badger's body, head, ears, and tail, see **Patterns**.

BADGER'S BODY & HEAD CONSTRUCTION

To construct Badger's limbs and torso, see **Basic Body**. Badger's unique head can be found in this chapter. For information on making strong seams and stuffing, see **Basic Techniques**.

MATERIALS

The **You Will Need** list includes a combination of items from both the **Basic Sewing Kit** and **Creative Materials**. Refer to **Tools & Materials** to learn about everything listed.

YOU WILL NEED

FOR BADGER'S HEAD AND BODY

- Charcoal felt, 15 x 17cm (6 x 6¾in)
- White felt, 17 x 6cm (6¾ x 2½in)
- 6-stranded embroidery floss (thread) to match the felt
- 6 extra-plush cotton pipe cleaners, 30cm (12in) long, *or* 8 regular craft-store chenille stems (pipe cleaners)
- Pipe cleaner folding template, size large (see **Basic Body** and **Patterns**)
- Wool stuffing 7–8g (5–6g for the head and 2g for the torso)*
- Acrylic paint: black and white
- No. 4 flat tipped or angled shader paint brush (or similar size)
- No. 6 round paint brush (or similar size)
- Waterproof fineliner pen, black, size 005 (0.2mm)
- Clear nail polish (optional)
- 2 sew-in eyes, 4mm (approx. ⅛in)
- Basic sewing kit (see **Tools & Materials**)

*Wool weight measurements are only a guide. Badger's belly should be soft and squeezable and his head firmly packed.

Gray shading is used to indicate the wrong side of the felt throughout the illustrations (see **Before You Begin**).

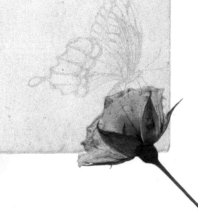

Body

Make a body (see **Basic Body**) in charcoal-colored felt (or another felt color of your choice) before assembling the head.

Head

MARK THE EYE PLACEMENT

1. With the paper pattern pieces still attached to the felt, lay the side-head pieces nose to nose on your work surface (**fig. 1a**).

2. Thread a needle with one strand of embroidery floss (thread) in any color—this marking stitch will be removed—and make a starting knot at one end. Stitch from front to back through the white dot in the center of each eye (**fig. 1b**). Knot the thread on the wrong side. Remove the paper pattern, popping the knot through the paper as you do so.

STITCH THE DARTS

The V-shaped cuts in the side-head pieces are called darts (see **Basic Techniques**).

1. Thread a needle with one strand of matching floss (thread) and make a starting knot at one end.

2. Each side-head piece has three darts: one on the top of the head (**fig. 1c**), one at the nose (**fig. 1d**), and one at the chin (**fig. 1e**). Begin by pinching the first dart, matching the sides of the V-shape. Whipstitch from the base of the V to the edge (**fig. 1f**). Repeat this process on the nose and chin darts.

3. After completing the three darts on the first side-head piece, repeat on the opposite side-head piece (**fig. 1g**).

STITCH THE CENTER SEAM

1. Thread a needle with one strand of matching floss and make a starting knot at one end.

2. Match the two side-head pieces with right sides together, and use a pin or wonder clip to hold the aligned darts in place (**fig. 1h**). Whipstitch the seam following the dashed line and knot off a few stitches beyond the dart.

3. Carefully turn the head right side out. Use the blunt end of a bamboo skewer or a pair of needle-nosed pliers to assist in turning. Whipstitch the back of the head closed following the dashed line, leaving the neck hole open (**fig. 1i**).

> Avoid catching your needle on the ending knots (✱) when you stitch the center seam (**fig. 1f**) by setting them back from the edge of the felt (see **Basic Techniques**).

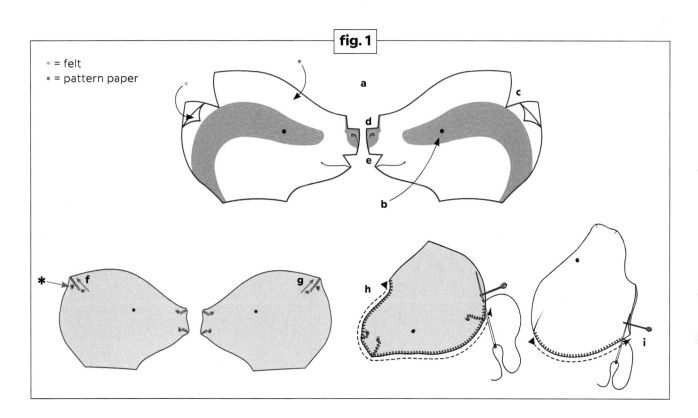

fig. 1

• = felt
• = pattern paper

fig. 2

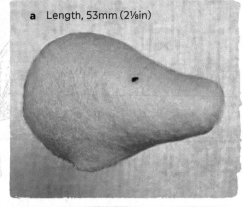

a Length, 53mm (2⅛in)

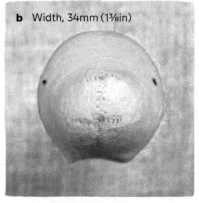

b Width, 34mm (1⅜in)

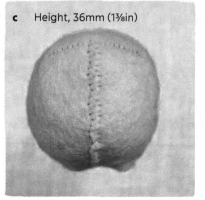

c Height, 36mm (1⅜in)

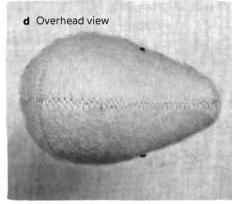

d Overhead view

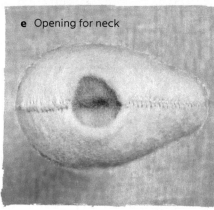

e Opening for neck

Head-size guide

As you fill and shape the head with stuffing, place it on top of each image until it matches the shape and size shown.

Each head will vary slightly in size, so use these images and approximate measurements as a rough guide.

STUFF THE HEAD

On Badger's face, the nose and chin darts help form his long flat muzzle, but sometimes, the muzzle can look too rounded after stuffing. Simply squeeze the stuffed muzzle from top to bottom to flatten it and correct the shape. See **fig. 2** in this chapter for Badger's dimensions.

Refer to **Basic Body** for more advice on stuffing heads.

FINISH THE HEAD

To complete the head, see **Basic Body**, which tells you how to:

- Attach the head
- Disguise the seams
- Prepare the surface

Face

Before preparing its surface for painting the face, attach the head to the body (see **Basic Body**). Refer to **Tools & Materials** to learn more about the different options for face painting.

PAINT THE HEAD

1. On each side of the head, mark a swooping line that passes through the eye hole, then one above and one below it that mark the the outer edges of the stripe (**fig. 1a**). Each line will meet at the back seam line (**fig. 1b**). Adjust the lines until you are happy with them (these will be covered with black paint). **Fig. 1c** shows the front view.

2. To make the lines on either side of the head symmetrical, check your progress from the sides, back, and front (**fig. 3a–c**).

3. With undiluted black acrylic paint, fill the stripes from the center-line outward, then create neat edges by using the flat or angled edge of your brush (**fig. 3d**). The stripes will form a V shape at the back of the head (**fig. 3e**). Leave to dry.

4. Use a pencil to mark the chin patch. Paint it as you did the stripes (**fig. 3f**) and leave to dry.

5. Check the head from all directions and make any final adjustments. When the paint has dried completely, refine the edges with a waterproof fineliner pen as needed.

fig. 3

Badger

Before you begin marking Badger's stripes, mark a stripe on a piece of pre-stiffened scrap felt and paint it with black acrylic paint to check how crisp you can make the edges. If needed, try adjusting the edges with a waterproof fineliner pen.

A soft white eraser can remove light pencil lines from the hairspray-stiffened felt. Avoid colored erasers as they may leave colored residue in the felt fibers.

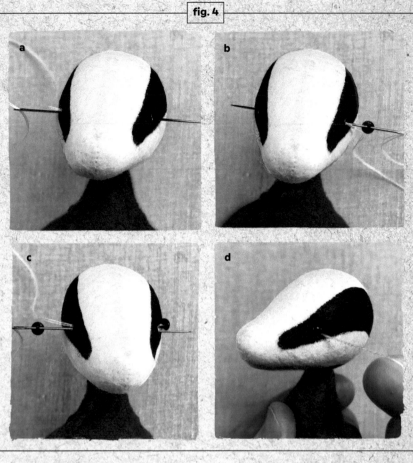

fig. 4

a

b

c

d

ATTACH THE EYES

1. Thread a long darning needle with two strands of white floss (thread) and make a knot in one end. Pass the needle through the head from right to left to lodge the knot in the interior stuffing. Then pass the needle back through to the opposite side to fully secure the knot in the head (**fig. 4a**).

2. Thread the needle through the shaft of the first sew-in eye, then pass the needle through the head from right to left (**fig. 4b**).

3. Add the second eye, then pass the needle through to the opposite side (**fig. 4c**). Repeat, catching each eye shaft one more time.

4. Pull the floss (thread) taut to indent the eyes (**fig. 4d**), then knot off. Insert the needle under the eye (exiting anywhere) and pull through to pop the knot below the eye.

PAINT THE FACE

Painting Badger's nose may seem fiddly, but the process is surprisingly simple; and if you need a fresh start, it is just a paint layer away.

1. Prepare the paint. In addition to using black and white straight from the tube, mix two shades of gray: charcoal and a lighter gray (**fig. 5a**). Add as little water as possible as you mix. Clean the brush and remove excess water on a paper towel.

2. Draw the nose lightly in pencil, then trace the outline with the black fineliner pen (**fig. 5b**).

3. Repeat for the vertical connecting line and Badger's smile (**fig. 5c**).

4. Use the clean No. 6 brush, dampened and brought to a point, to fill in the nose with black paint (**fig. 5d**). Leave to dry a little.

5. Clean the brush, remove excess water, and bring the tip to a point. Fill in the center of the nose with the lighter gray paint, leaving an outer black margin (**fig. 5e**). Use the charcoal paint to blend the gray into the black margin. Leave to dry.

6. To create the nostrils, first mark them in with the black fineliner pen (**fig. 5f**).

7. Water down the white paint slightly and mix well. Clean the brush and reshape. Use the tip to highlight the top and bottom of the nostrils (**fig. 5g**). If you overdo it, use a damp paper towel to remove the white and repeat.

8. Clean and reshape the brush, then paint dashes of gray onto Badger's black stripes.

9. With a black or sepia fineliner pen, mark in whisker dots on Badger's muzzle.

fig. 5

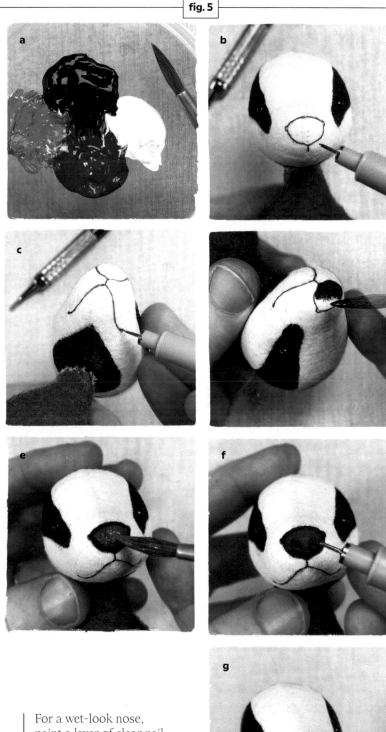

For a wet-look nose, paint a layer of clear nail polish onto the nose for a shiny final effect!

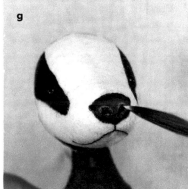

Badger

MAKE & ATTACH THE EARS

1. Lay out the charcoal-felt ears pieces side by side. Hold on to the square "tab" side of the first white-felt patch and apply a thin bead of tacky glue to its curved edge. Spread the glue in a thin layer over the curved edge. Using the shaded semi-circles on the paper pattern as a guide, place the curved edge of the white patch over the curved edge of the gray ear. Create the opposite ear in the same way (**fig. 6a**).

2. Cut away the excess white-felt tabs, trimming flush to the charcoal edge (**fig. 6b**).

3. Fray the curved and straight edges of both ears. To do this, use a pin to prick the felt edge and pull it outward to break up the wool fibers and soften the cut edge (**fig. 6c**). Pull off any loose fibers and pills for a uniformly fringed edge.

4. Pin the ears to either side of the head, positioning them just below the top head darts, with the white patches facing the back of the head (**fig. 6d and e**).

5. Remove one ear and spread a thin layer of tacky glue along its flat-fringed edge (**fig 6f**). Using the pinned ear as a guide, glue the ear to the side of the head. As you do, curve the glue edge slightly, matching its fringy corners up with the outer edges of the black stripe. Repeat to attach the opposite ear and allow to dry completely.

6. Thin out a small amount of black paint into a watery wash, then brush it onto the back-side of the ear, blending the glued fringe into the painted stripe. Using the same black paint wash, add paint to the inside of the ear, leaving the fringed edge soft and free of paint (**fig. 6g**).

fig. 6

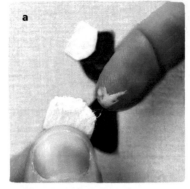
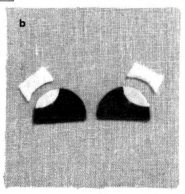
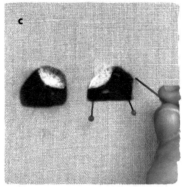

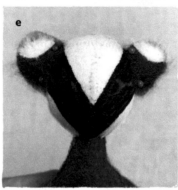

Due to their "tufted" nature, the ear corners may need an additional spot of glue to hold them down. Use the end of a pin to apply a tiny dab under each corner, then press down to adhere. Allow the glue to dry.

Badger

MAKE & ATTACH THE TAIL

1. Cut a length of pipe cleaner approx. 10cm (4in) long—a single length of either plush or chenille stem will work.

2. Prepare the pipe cleaner as follows: fold up one end by 3cm (1¼in). At the other end, use scissors to remove the cotton fluff above the 3cm (1¼in) fold, trimming the fiber down to the wire (see **Tools & Materials**). Fold over the trimmed end by approx. 5mm (¼in) (**fig. 7a**). Combined with trimming the fiber, this will allow the pipe cleaner to slide into the body and tail tube. (Standard chenille stems may be fine without trimming.)

3. Lay the two tail pieces on top of each other. Thread a needle with one strand of floss (thread) to match the tail and knot one end. Hide the starting knot between the felt layers at point A, then whipstitch around the curve to point B, leaving the flat end open (**fig. 7b**).

4. Insert the 3cm (1¼in) folded end of the pipe cleaner into the open end of the tail, leaving the trimmed top end exposed. Stuff the tail with small pinches of fiber. Avoid filling too firmly, as it will lose its bendability. Thread your needle with two strands of floss (thread) to match the tail and make a starting knot at one end. Gather the open end with a running stitch (**fig. 7c**), then tighten the floss (thread) to close the hole.

5. Locate the tail marking on the body, then make a channel for the tail's pipe cleaner by poking a hole (with the sharp end of a bamboo skewer) up into the torso. Make the hole up to where the arms cross.

6. Insert the exposed pipe cleaner up into the torso channel (**fig. 7d**). Thread your needle with two strands of floss (thread) and use a blind stitch (see **Basic Techniques**) to attach the tail to the body. As you stitch, bend the tail as needed to gain access to the seam. When you have made two passes of stitching around the tail, make and hide an ending knot.

Badger

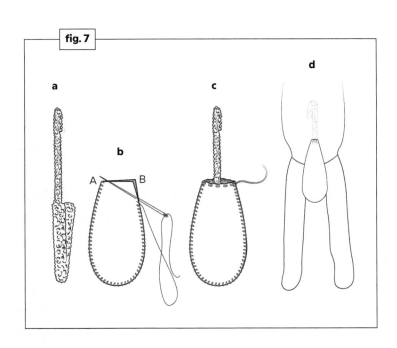

fig. 7

a

b

A   B

c

d

73

Badger's Outfit

His dressing gown
and nightcap embody
Badger's warm welcome
and tranquil home.

BADGER'S PATTERNS

For the pattern pieces for Badger's
dressing gown and nightcap, see
Patterns.

BADGER'S DRESSING GOWN

Read through the instructions here first,
then see **Basic Jacket**. The detailing
described in this section (painted stems
and leaves, stitched border, waist belt,
and back belt) can be completed before
you embark on the assembly of the
dressing gown itself.

BADGER'S NIGHTCAP

All the instructions for the nightcap are
included in this chapter.

YOU WILL NEED

FOR BADGER'S OUTFIT

- Sunset-orange felt (dressing gown),
  17 x 22cm (6¾ x 8¾in)

- Teal felt (night cap), 14 x 11cm (5½ x 4¼in)

- 6-stranded embroidery floss (thread),
  1 skein each in sunset and teal
  tones to match the felt colors

- Sage-green fiber (nightcap tassel). Use
  crewel or cotton embroidery floss (thread)
  or a fine yarn of your choice. The finished
  tassel will be trimmed to about 15mm
  (⅝in) long, so not much fiber is needed.

- Waterproof fineliner pen,
  black, size 005 (0.2mm)

- Acrylic paint pens: gold, 0.7mm and green,
  0.7mm (or a fine brush, gold and sage
  green acrylic paint, and a drop of dish soap
  (washing up liquid): see **Tools & Materials**)

- Basic sewing kit (see **Tools & Materials**)

See the **Tools & Materials** section for more
information about everything in Badger's
You Will Need list.

Badger's dressing gown is handsomely detailed,
but the robe is so cozy and smart it stands on
its own without the leafy frills. If you are an avid
embroiderer, consider stitching the leaf pattern,
or add contrasting tasseled ends to the waist belt
to match the nightcap, or roomy front pockets
for carrying a small book or bedtime snacks.

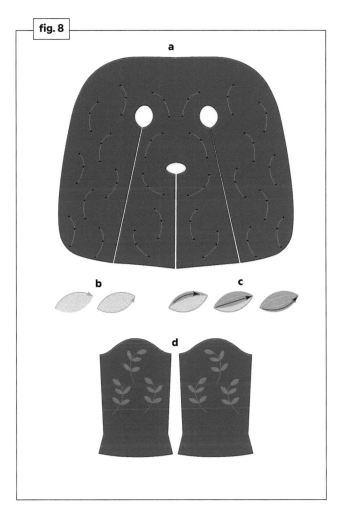

fig. 8

a

b   c

d

TO PREPARE

Cut the pattern pieces for Badger's dressing gown and nightcap from the felt (see **Patterns**). Make sure you cut along the additional dotted cutting lines as indicated on the paper pattern *before* you proceed with detailing and assembly.

Dressing gown

Refer to **Basic Jacket** for assembly instructions after completing the detailing below.

LEAF PATTERN

Unlike his head, the felt for Badger's dressing gown and nightcap is *not* treated with hairspray. As a result, the acrylic paint pens will lift the fibers a bit as you work, but this is normal. Experiment on untreated scrap felt to get a feel for the pens. I hold the pens at an angle to the felt for a smoother result. The exact angle may vary between brands. Shake and prime the pen as necessary while you work. See **Tools & Materials** to learn more about paint pens.

1. Stem placement: With the paper pattern pieces still attached to the felt, use a sharp skewer to poke holes through the paper at the ends and midpoint of each stem. Then poke the nib of a black waterproof fineliner pen through each hole to mark the placement on the felt with a small dot (**fig. 8a**). Remove the paper patterns.

2. The stems: The illustration shows fine white lines as the stem placement (**fig. 8a**). With the fine-nib gold acrylic paint pen, draw each stem using the three black dots as your guide to creating a curve. Angle the pen and pivot the felt to maintain the direction of each curve. Allow the paint to dry before moving on to the leaves.

3. The leaves: Use the pattern as a reference for placement (one at the top of each stem and two pairs along the length). First, make two pen strokes for the outline (**fig. 8b**), then fill in the center with two or three more strokes (**fig. 8c**). Again, angle the pen and pivot the felt as you draw. Complete the body and sleeves in this way (**fig. 8d**).

> The leaves will not have extra-crisp edges as a natural result of painting on a fibrous surface. I like the softly aged and painterly appearance it gives the fabric.

BORDER

The dashed line around the outer edge of the paper pattern indicates the running-stitch border (see **Basic Techniques**).

Thread your needle with two strands of floss (thread) and make a starting knot at one end. Stitch the border around the front edge of the garment approx. 2mm (1/16in) from its edge (**fig. 9**). Follow the red arrows from **A** to **B**, then knot off on the back of the garment. Thread your needle again as before and complete the running-stitch border on the back of the garment. Follow the blue arrows from **C** to **D**, then knot off again on the back side.

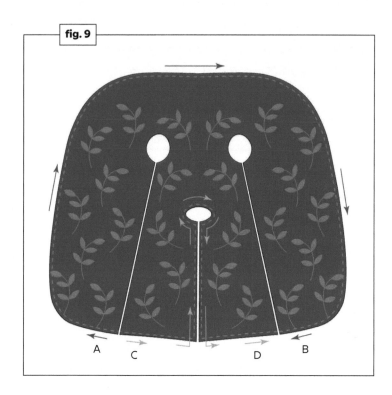

fig. 9

A   C   D   B

WAIST & BACK BELT

1. The waist belt pattern is split into two pieces with a central connection point. If you have a long piece of felt, you can join the paper pattern pieces with tape and cut the belt as one unit. If not, whipstitch the square ends of the belt together (**fig. 10a**) with a single strand of matching floss (thread), then knot off to end the stitch.

2 Thread a needle with two strands of contrasting teal floss (thread) or a color of your choice and make a starting knot at one end. Make the belt border with a small running stitch (see **Basic Techniques**) around the edges 1.5 to 2mm (1/16in) from the edge.

3 Orient the center point of the belt just above the tail hole on the back side of the dressing gown and pin the

belt in place. Make a few small basting (tacking) stitches (see **Basic Techniques**) to attach the belt to the garment. Make starting and ending knots on the wrong side of the dressing gown or beneath the belt.

4. The tail-belt (**fig. 10b**) is finished with a buttonhole stitch border (see **Basic Techniques**). Thread a needle with a single strand of contrasting orange floss (thread) or a color of your choice and stitch around the edge, making starting and ending knots on the same side. Orient the tail-belt under the tail hole. Attach the belt to the garment with basting (tacking) stitches (See **Basic Techniques**) through the center point of either end.

The crisp and fresh dressing gown looks lovely, but you can also create the soft, rumpled look of cozy hibernation! Spritz the robe with water and scrunch it up in a towel to remove any excess water. Lay flat and remove any sharp wrinkles to leave the surface soft and textured.

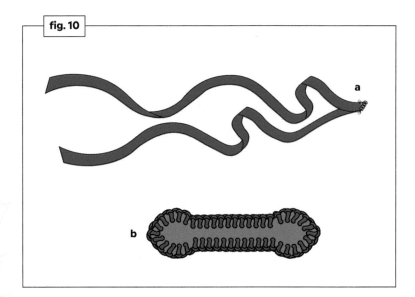

fig. 10

a

b

Badger

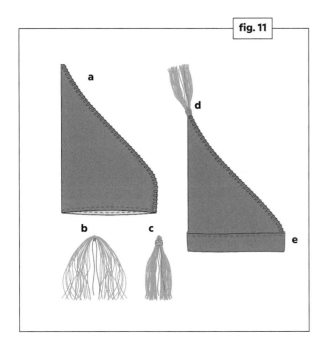

fig. 11

a

d

b   c   e

Nightcap

1. Thread a needle with two strands of sunset-orange floss (thread) and make a starting knot at one end. Make a running-stitch border on the flat side about 2mm (approx. ⅟₁₆in) from the edge. Make starting and ending knots on the outside.

2. Thread a needle with one strand of teal floss (thread) and make a starting knot at one end. Referring to the pattern, fold the cap in half on the center-front fold line. With the starting knot on the outside, whipstitch the sloped side to the pointed end (**fig. 11a**). Hide the ending knot.

3. For the tassel, wrap the fiber around two fingers, eight times . Remove your fingers and cut the loop open. Cut a length of fiber to bind the bundle at its center with a square knot (right over left, then left over right). Fold the bundle in half, hiding the knot between the fibers (**fig. 11b**).

4. Thread a needle with one strand of matching floss (thread) and wrap it tightly several times around the folded end to secure (**fig. 11c**). Stitch back and forth through the wrapped thread a few times, with last stitch directed downward. Cut the thread to match the fringe.

5. Using one strand of sunset-orange floss (thread), whipstitch the folded end of the tassel to the top of the hat, then wrap tightly several times around the base to create a contrasting band of color between the hat and tassel (**fig. 11d**). Cut and knot off the floss (thread), and hide the knot. Fold up the bottom edge of the cap (**fig. 11e**). Trim the tassel to the length of your choice.

6. As you did with the dressing gown, spritz the hat with water and scrunch. While still damp, place on Badger's head with the seam at the back. Fold down the point to one side and pin in place to the folded brim until dry to hold the shape.

Badger

Toad

I think Ratty says it best. Toad is always good-tempered, always glad to see you, always sorry to see you go! He is simple, good-natured, and affectionate. Although sometimes boastful and conceited, Ratty knows that his dear friend Toady also has some great qualities. In this classic story, Toad is full of enthusiasm, with new adventures and catastrophes around every bend. His dapper felt outfits reflect his outlook, mixing an eye-catching teal waistcoat with bold scarlet pants and shiny patent shoes. I like to think that over the last one hundred (plus) years, Toad's boastful and conceited ways have matured, mellowed, and modernized. Today, stitched dapperly in colorful felt, young imaginations can channel Toads' best self, with his good temper and adventurous soul.

"Hooray!" he cried, jumping up on seeing them, "this is splendid!" He shook the paws of both of them warmly, never waiting for an introduction to the Mole. "How kind of you!" he went on, dancing round them. "I was just going to send a boat down the river for you, Ratty, with strict orders that you were to be fetched up here at once, whatever you were doing. I want you badly—both of you. Now what will you take? Come inside and have something! You don't know how lucky it is, your turning up just now!"

Making Toad

TOAD'S PATTERNS

For the pattern pieces for Toad's body and head, see **Patterns**.

TOAD'S BODY & HEAD CONSTRUCTION

To assemble Toad's body and arms, see **Basic Body**. Toad's unique head and limb construction can be found in this chapter. For information on making strong seams and stuffing, see **Basic Techniques**.

TOAD'S EYES & SHOES

Toad's unique eye construction and painted shoes can be found in this chapter.

MATERIALS

The **You Will Need** list includes a combination of items from both the **Basic Sewing Kit** and **Creative Materials**. Refer to **Tools & Materials** to learn about everything listed.

YOU WILL NEED

FOR TOAD'S HEAD & BODY

- Relish green felt (body), 18 x 23cm (7 x 9½in) (or another felt color of your choice)
- White felt (eyes), 7 x 4cm (2¾in x 1⅝in)
- 6-stranded embroidery floss (thread) in colors to match the felt
- 5 extra-plush cotton pipe cleaners, 30cm (12in) long, *or* 7 regular craft-store chenille stems (pipe cleaners)
- Wool stuffing, 3–4g (1–2g for the head, and 2g for the torso)*
- Waterproof fineliner pen, black, size 05 (0.45mm)
- Acrylic paint pen: white 0.7mm (or white acrylic paint and an extra-fine brush)
- Acrylic paint: black
- No. 6 round watercolor paint brush, or 6mm (¼in) angled shader brush
- Fine-grit sandpaper or an emery board
- Clear nail polish
- Basic sewing kit (see **Tools & Materials**)

*Wool weight measurements are only a guide. Toad's belly should be soft and squeezable and his head lightly packed.

fig. 1

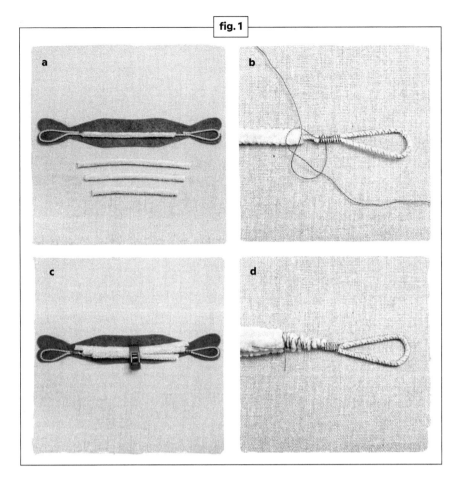

Arms & legs

Toad has a unique limb structure (legs and arms)—narrow wrists and ankles are combined with broad hands and feet. The limbs are filled primarily with pipe cleaners, except for a pinch of stuffing inside each hand and foot.

1. The leg and arm pieces are constructed using the same process. For each limb, cut one pipe cleaner to a length of 28cm (11in). Cut a second pipe cleaner into three lengths of 10.5cm (4⅛in), 9.5cm (3¾in), and 8.5cm (3⅜in) (measurements included as cutting guides in **Templates**.)

2. Trim off 9.5cm (3¾in) of cotton fluff from both ends of the 28cm (11in) pipe cleaner. (For removing fluff, see **Tools & Materials**.)

3. Center the trimmed 28cm (11in) pipe cleaner over the felt. Using the template as a guide, bend each end of the trimmed portion to fit within the rounded ends of the felt piece (**fig. 1a**). Remove from the felt and tightly wrap the ends just above the loop with a single strand of embroidery floss (thread) (**fig. 1b**). Make a square knot (right over left, then left over right) to secure.

4. Center and clip the three graduated pipe cleaners on top of the bent and bound pipe-cleaner (**fig. 1c**). Tightly wrap the cut ends of the graduated pipe cleaners just above the loop at either end of the bundle (**fig. 1d**).

fig. 2

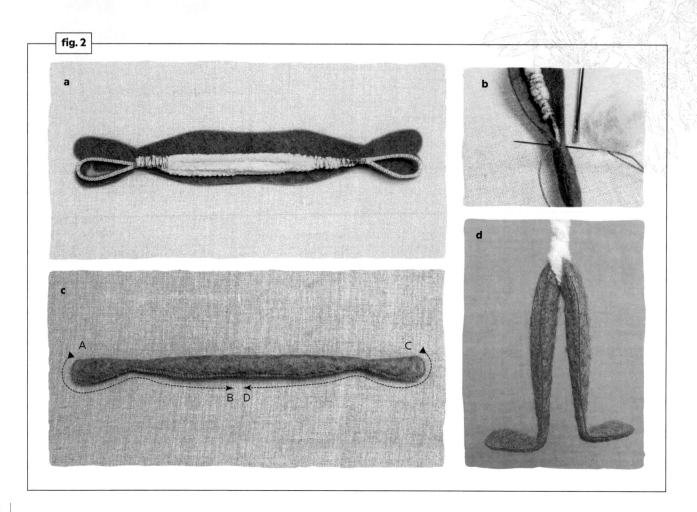

5. Lay the finished pipe cleaner bundle on top of the first felt leg piece as shown (**fig. 2a**). Pinch the felt at the center point around the pipe cleaner bundle and secure it with a wonder clip. Thread a needle with a single strand of matching floss (thread) and make a starting knot at one end. Fold the first curved end around the looped pipe cleaner and hide the starting knot between the two felt layers. Begin whipstitching around the first curved "foot" end. Pause stitching shortly before reaching the ankle to insert a pinch of stuffing into the foot (**fig. 2b**), then continue whipstitching to point **B** (**fig. 2c**). Repeat on the opposite end from **C** to **D**, remembering to stuff the opposite foot.

6. Repeat steps 1–5 to create an identical limb structure. One will become the legs, and one will become the arms.

7. See **Basic Body** to complete Toad's body construction. The only difference for Toad is that the seams of his legs are positioned backward (like the seam on a pair of vintage stockings), as shown in red (**fig. 2d**).

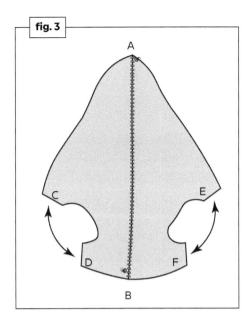

fig. 3

Head

Gray shading is used to indicate the wrong side of the felt throughout the illustrations (see **Before You Begin**).

ASSEMBLE THE TOP HEAD

1. Thread a needle with a single strand of green floss (thread) and make a starting knot one end. Whipstitch the left and right side-head pieces together along their center seam from **A** to **B** (**fig. 3**), with the starting and ending knots visible on the stitching side (wrong side).

2. Thread a needle with a single strand of matching floss and knot one end. Whipstitch the seam below the first eye by bringing together the short flat edges of points **C** and **D** and leaving the starting and ending knots visible on the stitching side (**fig. 3**). Repeat below the second eye by bringing together the short flat edges of points **E** and **F**.

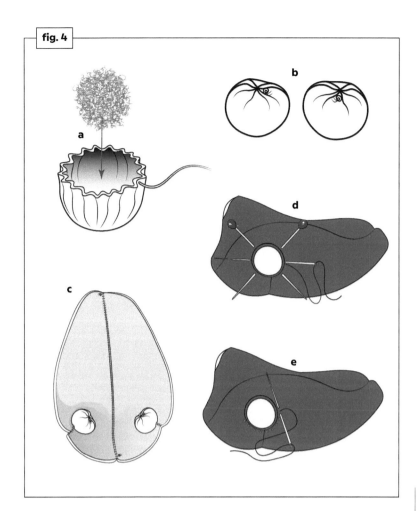

fig. 4

ASSEMBLE & ATTACH THE EYES

1. Thread a needle with two strands of white floss (thread) and make a starting knot at one end. Make a running stitch around the edge of the first white felt circle, leaving the needle and thread attached. Gather the edge of the circle to form a cup (**fig. 4a**).

2. Take a small pinch of stuffing and ball it up between your fingers to compress the fibers. Place inside the felt cup and draw in the thread to close. Make a few Whipstitches across the gathered opening to secure it. Repeat to make the second eyeball (**fig. 4b**).

3. Turn the top head right side out. Place the eyeballs into the eye holes *from the wrong side*. The gathered side of the eyeballs and all the stitching should be visible on the wrong side (**fig. 4c**).

4. Temporarily hold the eyeballs in place with two crossing pins (**fig. 4d**). Thread a needle with a single strand of contrasting floss (thread) and make a starting knot at one end. For easier stitching, replace the pins with two temporary stitches (one horizontal and one vertical) and leave the starting and ending knots on the outside for easy removal.

5. Thread a needle with a single strand of green floss (thread) and and make a starting knot at one end. Make a backstitch around the edge of the eye hole, catching the eyeball below with every stitch (**fig. 4e**).

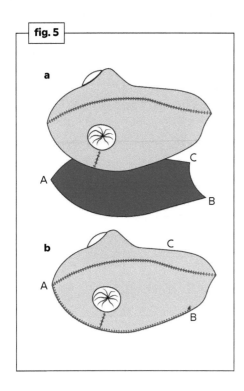

fig. 5

a

A

C

B

b

A

C

B

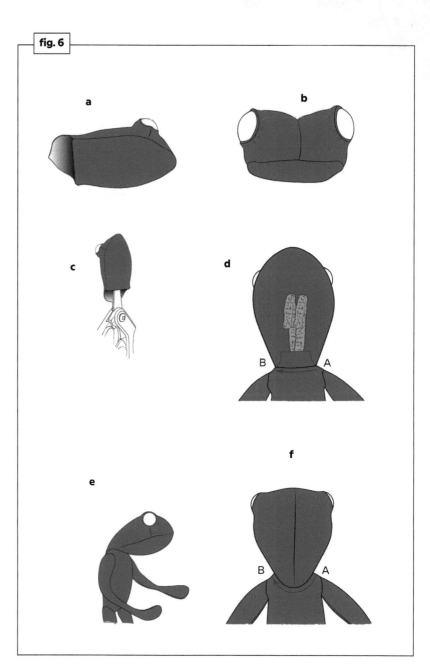

fig. 6

a

b

c

d

B A

e

f

B A

ATTACH THE CHIN

1. Turn the top head wrong side out and lay it over the chin piece (shown right side up) (**fig. 5a**).

2. Thread a needle with a single strand of matching green floss (thread) and make a starting knot at one end. Whipstitch from **A** to **B**, then knot off on the wrong side of the felt. Begin again at **A** and whipstitch to **C**, knotting off as before (**fig. 5b**).

STUFF & ATTACH THE HEAD

1. Use a bamboo skewer or needle-nosed pliers to help turn the head right side out (side bottom view **fig. 6a**, front view **fig. 6b**).

2. Toad's head is not densely packed like those of the other animals. Instead, loosely fill the front half of the head with stuffing, leaving the open-ended half empty. This space will allow you to bend the head down at the neck. More stuffing can be added as necessary later in the process. Cut a channel up into the head stuffing (**fig. 6c**). Slip the head over the neck vertically, sliding the pipe cleaner into the stuffing channel (**fig. 6d**).

3. Thread a needle with two strands of floss (thread) and knot one end. Hide the starting knot in the neck felt at point **A**. Use a blind stitch (see **Basic Techniques**) to connect the front edge of the head to the body from **A** to **B** (**fig. 6d**).

4. Before stitching the back of the head, fold the neck down from its vertical position (**fig. 6e**). Now it is time to add more stuffing to either side of the head to fill out the cheeks, and a small amount at the back of the head.

5. To finish attaching the head to the body, continue to blind stitch on the back of the neck from **A** back to **B** (**fig. 6f**). Make an ending knot and hide.

Toad

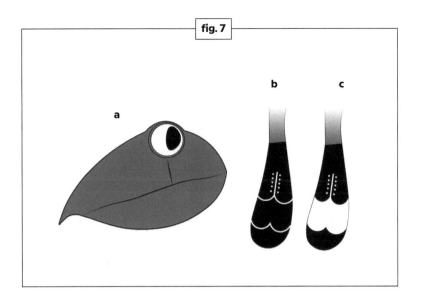

fig. 7

a b c

Toad has some fancy feet, and they're well worth the extra effort, but you might like to keep it simple. Perhaps Toad has his eye on a pair of colorful galoshes from the accessories section (which won't fit over his wingtips). No problem! Simply construct Toad with the legs and arms pieces shown in the Basic Body section (used for Ratty and Badger). He might not be ready for town but can happily enjoy a walk along the river bank with friends or take in some boating.

Paint the eyes & shoes

1. Apply non-aerosol hairspray to the eyeballs and the feet with a soft paint brush to prepare the surface for painting. Cover the white surface of each eye, and the tops and bottoms of the feet up to the ankles. Allow to dry completely.

2. Turn an iron up to high and sit it upright on your work surface. Carefully press and rotate the white of the eyeball onto the iron to smooth the felt's surface. Repeat on each foot, smoothing the surface on the top, bottom, and side edges.

3. For the eye, use a pencil to lightly sketch the outline of a forward-facing pupil. Color in the pupil with a black fineliner pen or a small brush and black acrylic paint (**fig. 7a**).

4. For the black underlayer of the wing tips, use an angled shader brush and black acrylic paint straight from the tube—do not add any water. Paint from the ankles down on the top and bottom of the feet. Allow the paint to dry completely. For an extra-smooth surface, use fine-grit sandpaper or the fine side of an emery board to remove any roughness. Sand the tops, bottoms, and sides of the painted feet, then add a second coat of paint and allow it to dry completely.

5. Use a white fine-tip acrylic paint pen to make two rounded W shapes. Centered above the top W, add a vertical line and lacing holes (**fig. 7b**).

6. Paint the space between the W shapes with white acrylic paint or a paint pen (**fig. 7c**). (Paint pens may need additional coats due to their thinner consistency.) For a patent-leather effect, paint the black tips with clear nail polish.

Toad

85

Toad's Outfit

Always the dapper chap, Toad's tailcoat is perfect paired with his smart wingtips.

TOAD'S PATTERNS

For the pattern pieces for Toad's tailcoat, vest, and pants see **Patterns**.

TOAD'S TAILCOAT

Read through the instructions here first, then see **Basic Jacket**. Much of the detailing described in this section (tab-cuff buttons and topstitching) can be completed before you embark on the jacket assembly itself.

TOAD'S VEST (WAISTCOAT)

All the instructions for Toad's vest (waistcoat) can be found in this chapter.

TOAD'S PANTS

See **Basic Pants** for the construction of the design. Tab-cuff buttons can be added either before or after assembly.

YOU WILL NEED

FOR TOAD'S OUTFIT

- Warm-gray felt (tailcoat), 18 x 14cm (7 x 5½in)

- Red felt (pants), 16cm x 10cm (6¼ x 4in)

- Dark-teal felt (vest), 12 x 7cm (4¾ x 2¾in)

- 6-stranded embroidery floss (thread) in gray, red, and dark teal tones to match the felt colors

- 8 buttons, antique bronze, 4mm (approx. ⅛in)

- 2 snaps, antique bronze, 6mm (approx. ¼in)

- Basic sewing kit (see **Tools & Materials**)

See the **Tools & Materials** section for more information about everything in Toad's **You Will Need** list.

TO PREPARE

Cut the pattern pieces for Toad's clothes from the felt (see **Patterns**). You will find patterns for his tailcoat, vest (waistcoat) and pants.

Tailcoat

On the warm-gray felt pieces, complete the detailing (whipstitch, running stitch, lazy daisy and French knot) as follows. Then for the main construction of the tailcoat, see **Basic Jacket**.

EMBROIDERY & BUTTONS

1. To make the running stitch borders on the tailcoat, thread your needle with two strands of dark teal floss (thead), or a color of your choice, and make a starting knot at one end. Stitch around the perimeter of the coat, the sleeve cuffs, and the curved sides of the center-back tail. On the top edge of the pockets, use only one strand (**fig. 1**). Make all starting and ending knots on the same side of the felt (the side with the knots will become the wrong side).

2. To make the decorative stitches on the back of the coat, thread your needle with two strands of green floss (thread) and make a starting knot at one end. Stitch lazy daisy stitches (**fig. 1a**) and French knots (**fig. 1b**) or a stitch combination of your choice (see **Basic Techniques**). Make all starting and ending knots on the wrong side.

3. Thread a needle with a single strand of matching floss (thead) and knot one end. Center and stitch one button to each of the coat's tab-cuff sleeves (**fig. 1c**).

POCKETS

Thread a needle with a single strand of dark teal floss (thread) and knot one end. Position the pockets on the sides of the coat (see the pattern for placement) and attach them to the coat with a running stitch around their sides. Make all starting and ending knots on the wrong side.

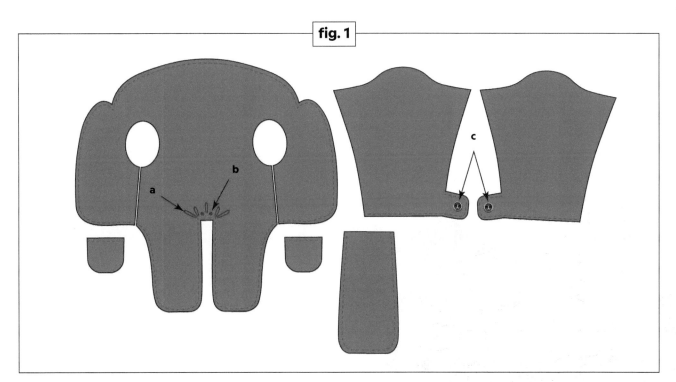

fig. 1

CENTER-BACK TAIL

Thread a needle with a single strand of gray floss (thread) and make a starting knot at one end. Lay down the coat wrong side up. Center the tail over the back split, aligning its curved bottom edge with the tails on the main coat piece (**fig. 2**). Whipstitch the flat top edge of the tail to the coat. Make the stitches through *the felt surface only* so that they are not visible on the right side of the coat.

FINISH THE TAILCOAT

To set in the sleeves and stitch the side seams, see **Basic Jacket**. This tailcoat is designed to be worn open, with no front closure.

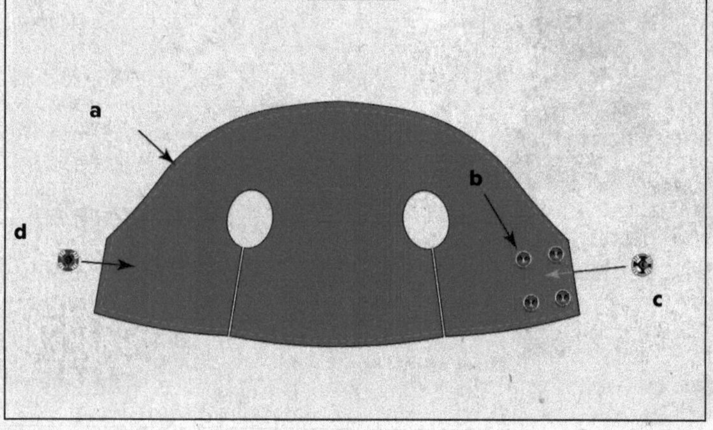

Vest (waistcoat)

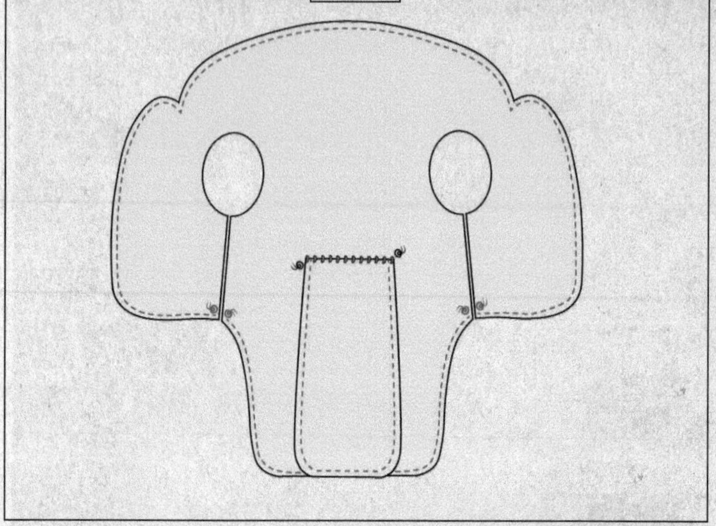

1. Follow *Embroidery & Buttons, step 1,* to make the running stitch border (**fig. 3a**).

2. Use the pattern as a guide for button placement (**fig. 3b**). Thread a needle with a single strand of matching floss (thread) and knot one end. Stitch on the buttons with starting and ending knots on the wrong side of the vest.

3. To attach the nipple side of the snap (**fig. 3c**), thread your needle with a single strand of matching floss (thread) and make a starting knot at one end. Stitch the snap to the wrong side of the vest (waistcoat), centered between the four buttons. Make the stitches through the felt surface only so that they are not visible on the right side of the coat (see **Basic Techniques**).

4. To stitch the side seams, thread your needle with a single strand of floss (thread) to match the felt and knot one end. Turn the garment to the wrong side, matching the side seams. Whipstitch the side seams, making the starting and ending knots on the wrong side.

5. To attach the dimple side of the snap (**fig. 3d**), thread your needle with one strand of matching floss and make a starting knot at one end. Fit the vest (waistcoat) to Toad, overlapping the front placket. Press the nipple side of the snap into the felt below to make an indentation. Center and stitch the dimple side of the snap to the indentation; make starting and ending knots on the wrong side of the felt.

6. For an optional folded collar, press down its edge with a hot iron, using the dashed fold line on the pattern as your guide.

fig. 2

fig. 3

Pants

1. Refer to **Basic Pants** chapter and attach the nipple side of the snap as directed.

2. To stitch the first side seam, thread your needle with a single strand of matching floss (thread) and make a starting knot at one end. Whipstitch the seam from the waist down to the tab cuff. Open the seam to the right side, flipping the tab to the front of the seam (**fig. 4a**). Center and stitch the button (or a black super-duo bead—see the car photo) onto the tab with the remaining thread on your needle. Stitch through the button and both layers of felt several times to secure the button, then knot off on the wrong side.

3. Fold the pants along the stitched side seam, with right sides together. Whipstitch the opposite side seam down to the tab. Turn the pants tube right side out, then flip the remaining tab to the front (**fig. 4b**). Center and stitch its button onto the tab cuff.

4. Refer to **Basic Pants** to stitch the inseam and attach the dimple side of the snap.

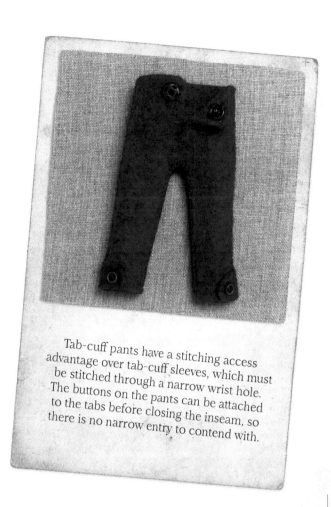

Tab-cuff pants have a stitching access advantage over tab-cuff sleeves, which must be stitched through a narrow wrist hole. The buttons on the pants can be attached to the tabs before closing the inseam, so there is no narrow entry to contend with.

Toad

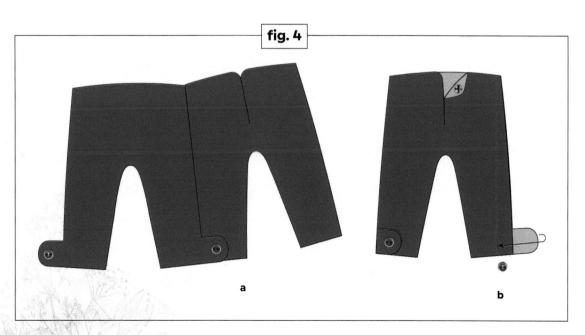

fig. 4

a

b

Accessories

With our felt characters and this charming collection of
accessories, the River Bank, Meadow, and Wild Wood adventures
will spring to life! No matter the season, a wingback chair by
the hearth fits into every animal's home, and given enough
playtime, the cozy felt slippers you make might even become
as down-in-the-heel as Badger's. Fancy a tiny pair of galoshes?
They're brilliant for mucking about by the River Bank and for
winter hikes into the Wild Wood (it's always good to be prepared
for snow!). Our characters' adventures would not be complete
without a proper notebook for penning verse, a dropline and fish
for lazy summer boating excursions, and a beautiful luncheon
basket to feast from, always with the very best of friends.

All the patterns you need are in the **Patterns** section,
while more details of the materials in the **You Will
Need** lists can be found in **Tools & Materials**.

When they got home, the Rat made a bright fire in the parlor, and planted the Mole in an arm-chair in front of it, having fetched down a dressing-gown and slippers for him, and told him river stories till supper-time.

Luncheon Basket

A picnic is only complete with a luncheon basket filled with delicious food, which Mole in particular gets very excited about!

Before you begin

Paper: This pattern must be printed onto freezer paper to create an iron-on pattern (see **Tools & Materials**).

Cutting tools: For accuracy, I recommend using a combination of a rotary cutter, utility knife, and small sharp-pointed scissors to cut the luncheon basket.

Preparing the felt and pattern

1. The day *before* you plan to make the basket, stiffen both colors of felt with hairspray.

Brush on or spray the hairspray onto the felt until the material is completely saturated. Lay it flat and let it dry overnight. (Place it on the plastic side of freezer paper or tin foil to stop the felt sticking to your worksurface.) When the felt pieces are completely dry, they should be evenly stiff without any soft spots—like a felt-cardboard hybrid material.

2. Cut out the pattern as follows.

From the printed freezer paper, cut:

- The solid rectangular border surrounding the luncheon basket pattern piece
- The solid outside edges of the two weaving strip panels
- The two straps
- The rectangles that surround each of the two side-handle pieces

From the chipboard, cut:

- The inside chipboard base

3. Iron the luncheon basket and weaving strip freezer-paper pattern pieces to the stiffened, dried felt. Cut between the basket piece and the weaving strips to separate them from each other. On the basket pattern piece, the area shaded with dots is *not* waste material—it will be utilized as interior corner brackets later in the project.

YOU WILL NEED

- Color 1 (heather-brown felt), 15 x 23cm (6 x 9in)
- Color 2 (chocolate felt), 5 x 7cm (2 x 2¾in)
- 6-stranded embroidery floss (thread) in matching browns
- Chipboard, 4 x 7cm (1½ x 2¾in)
- Fast-grabbing tacky glue (extra-thick, clear-drying, flexible glue)
- Wooden coffee stirrer (ideally 150 x 5 x 2mm / 6 x ³⁄₁₆ x ¹⁄₁₆in) or a slim wooden craft dowel
- Small, sharp-pointed scissors
- Adhesive tape (washi tape or other low-tack tape)
- Sandpaper or an emery board
- Basic sewing kit (see **Tools & Materials**)

Cutting the luncheon basket pieces

Use the following tools to cut the felt.

Rotary cutter: Using a non-slip ruler, cut along the *four dashed lines* around the outer edges of the top, sides, and front of the basket.

Scissors: Cut away the *polka dot* areas. Use the sharp tips of the scissors to cut clean, crisp interior corners. Save the scraps for the interior corner brackets.

Utility knife: Using a non-slip ruler, cut away the *small area shaded in red* along the sides of the basket's back panel. It is hard to get into these tiny interior corners with scissors or a roller cutter, but the utility knife is the perfect tool!

fig. 1

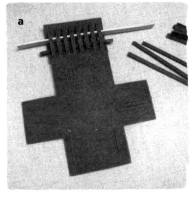

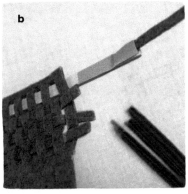

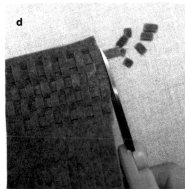

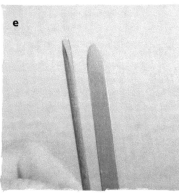

For smoother weaving, taper the leading end (sides and thickness) of the coffee stirrer (or slim wooden dowel) with sandpaper or an emery board (**fig.1e**).

1. Using a non-slip ruler and utility knife again, cut the interior "warp" lines, shown in red (on the template, each line has a red bar at the beginning and end of the cut). Cut inward, following the direction of the arrows so that you don't slip and cut through the outer edge of the basket. Go back in with your blade at the end of each cut to make sure that the cut reaches the bar at each end. Cut slowly and carefully, holding the ruler tightly so that nothing shifts as you cut. After cutting, remove the iron-on pattern piece.

2. Finally, cut the remaining pieces. Cut out the weaving strips with a ruler and rotary cutter, and the inside chipboard piece with a ruler and utility knife.

Weaving the top and back

1. Begin by weaving the top of the basket. Using the coffee stirrer, weave in and out through the cut warp, then turn the stirrer on its side to open the space between the strips (**fig. 1a**). Slide the first long weaving strip through the opening, then flip the stirrer down and use it to push the weaving strip down to the bottom of the warp cuts.

2. Repeat for the next two rows, alternating the weave pattern with each row. For the final row, weave through the stirrer as before (or use a slimmer wooden dowl as necessary). Tape the end of the weaving strip to the end of the weaving tool and pull it through (**fig. 1b**).

3. Glue the ends of the strips down, working one at a time (eight in total). Using a fine applicator for the fast-grabbing tacky glue (such as the tip of a skewer), lift each end and dab a little bit of tacky glue on the warp edge below it (**fig. 1c**). Press and hold for a few moments until the glue grabs. Trim the overhanging ends flush with the sides (**fig. 1d**).

4. Repeat the weaving process on the back of the basket, continuing to use the longer weaving strips.

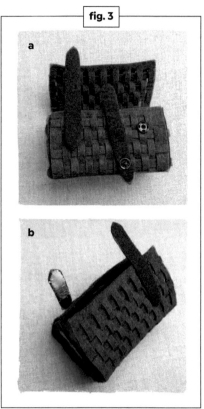

Weaving the sides and front

On the sides of the basket, your weave pattern should be the opposite of what you did on the back. For example, if the bottom row of the back begins with the weaving strip *over* the warp (**A**), start the side with the weaving strip *under* the warp (**B**) (**fig. 2a**). (If this is too fussy, don't worry—the basket will work fine without the alternating weave.)

Complete the opposite side and the front of the basket in the same manner.

Assembling the basket

1. Glue in the chipboard base of the basket (**fig. 2b**). You can paint the chipboard, or line it with decorative papers (or even a Liberty print adhesive sheet) for a cheery finishing touch!

2. To prepare the basket for the corner brackets, fold up the sides of the basket against the chipboard base and make a crease between the back and the cover. To make the L-shaped corner brackets, set your iron to high, and when ready, fold and press each of the reserved scrap pieces in half. Cut their folded widths to about 1cm (⅜in) wide (unfolded width 2cm / ¾in). Trim their heights to match the inside height of the basket.

3. Attach the two back-corner brackets one at a time. Spread glue over the *outside* surface of the corner bracket, then fit it to the inner back corner of the basket, bringing the side edges up to meet it (**fig. 2c**). Hold and press the corner to the bracket for a few minutes until the glue has grabbed. Some glues dry faster than others; I recommend using an extra-thick, fast-grabbing variety and testing it on a stiffened scrap of felt before applying it to your basket.

4. Before attaching the front brackets, sew on the front snaps. Thread a needle with a single strand of matching floss (thread) and make a starting knot at one end. Stitch the snap's dimple sides to the front of the basket, using the pattern as a reference for placement (**fig. 2d**).

Attaching the straps

1. Stitch the remaining snap sides to the end of each strap, using the pattern as a reference for placement. Thread a needle with a single strand of matching floss (thread) and make a starting knot at one end. Make the stitching through only the surface of the felt so that it will not show on the front side of the strap.

2. Snap the first strap to the front (**fig. 3a**), then bring it over the top of the basket, aligning it with the weave. Apply glue to the underside of the strap, then press it onto the top of the basket. Unsnap the front so that you can easily apply pressure, holding the layers together until the glue grabs. Repeat on the opposite strap (**fig. 3b**).

Attaching the handles

1. Fold and press (with a hot iron) the two side-handle rectangles (**fig. 4a**). Cut a 3mm strip with rounded ends (**fig. 4b**). Glue the center of the fold (from **A** to **B**), leaving the rounded ends unglued (**fig. 4c**). Curve the handle around your pinky finger or the shaft of a pen and allow to dry (**fig. 4d**). Glue handle points **C** and **D** to the sides of the basket halfway down (**fig. 4e**).

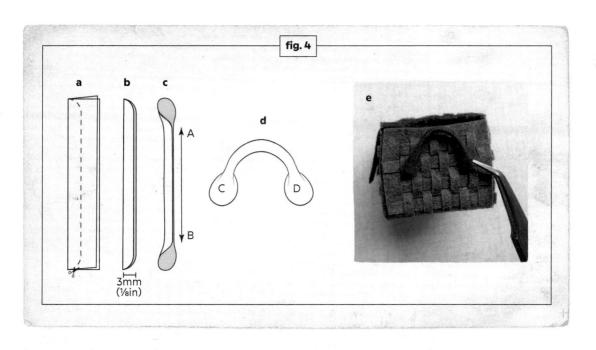

fig. 4

a   b   c

A

B

3mm
(⅛in)

d

C   D

e

Picnic Blanket

The friends can all sit together on this comfortable stitched blanket, whether enjoying a picnic or just lazing by the river on sunny day.

YOU WILL NEED

- Marble felt, 15 x 15cm (6 x 6in)
- 6-stranded embroidery floss (thread), 1 skein each in navy, teal, and chartreuse (or colors of your choice)
- Basic sewing kit (see **Tools & Materials**)

Because the buttonhole stitch uses up a lot of floss (thread), there need to be several connections. I've made this into a design detail by alternating the thread colors. Feel free to keep it simple and use only one color if you prefer. To neatly connect the first stitch of the new thread to the final stitch of the old thread, see **Basic Techniques**. For a soft rumpled look use the spritzing, scrunching and drying technique used to soften Badger's dressing gown.

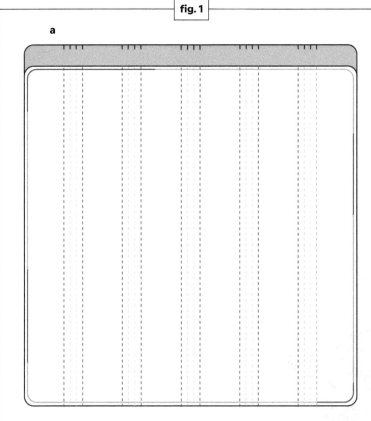

fig. 1

a

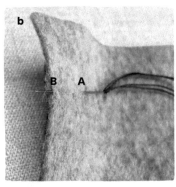

b

B A

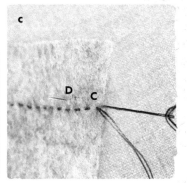

c

D C

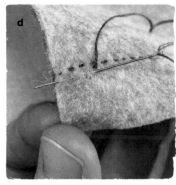

d

A quick alternative to stitching lines is to draw them! Mark the ends of the lines as described in step 1. Then use a ruler and colorful fine-tipped acrylic paint pens or waterproof fineliner pens to draw stripes. Buttonhole stitch the border or draw your own design there too.

Stitching the stripes

1. Cut the felt to match the pattern, then shift the pattern down to reveal the felt edge. Mark the ends of each line on the edge of the felt with a watersoluble pen or a discreet pencil mark (**fig. 1a**). Repeat on the opposite side of the blanket. Use the water-soluble pen or a chalk roller to connect the lines between the markings. If you use a chalk roller to join the lines, mark each line as you work because they fade as you handle the fabric.

2. The stripe colors can be ordered however you like. The stripes on my sample are ordered navy, teal, chartreuse, and navy. Thread a needle with a two-strand length of the first color (navy) and make a small knot at one end. Hide each starting knot by entering and sliding the needle (though only the felt's surface) from **A** to **B** (**fig. 1b**). Pull the thread just enough to pop the knot below the surface fibers. Reverse the direction of your needle and stitch the row of running stitches. For even stitches, make each stitch in two passes, front to back then back to front (rather than gathering several on the needle at one time).

3. At the end of the stitched line, hide the knot away from the edge as follows (**fig. 1c**): insert the needle through the edge at point **C** and through the surface of the felt, exiting at point **D** (to one side of the stitch line). Make an ending knot at the surface of the felt (**fig. 1d**) then slip the needle below the surface of the felt (and out the edge) just until the knot pops through. Repeat this process across the blanket, alternating your thread colors.

Stitching the border

1. Choose two of your coordinating colors to make the multicolored border. Thread a needle with two strands of your first color. Hide the starting knot below the surface of the felt, then begin the buttonhole stitch following the color chart on the edge of the pattern.

Fish & Drop Line

Life by the river means that fishing is a favorite pastime. Make the fishing drop line, then as many fish as you'd like to catch and eat!

YOU WILL NEED (FOR ONE FISH)

- Gold felt (body), 4 x 4cm (1½ x 1½in)
- Light blue felt (belly), 4 x 4cm (1½ x1½in)
- Pumpkin felt (fin), 2 x 3cm (¾ x 1⅛in)
- 6-stranded embroidery floss (thread) in shades to match the felt
- 2 glass seed-beads, green (eyes)
- 4 flat toothpicks
- Sandpaper or an emery board
- Basic sewing kit (see **Tools & Materials**)

For clarity in this project, the wrong sides are shown in color in the illustrations.

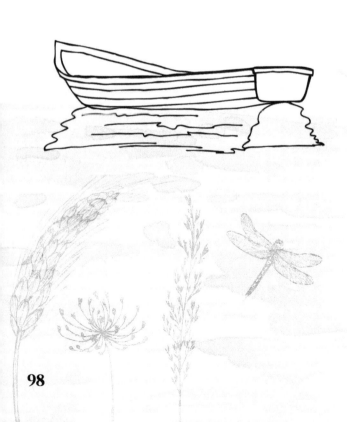

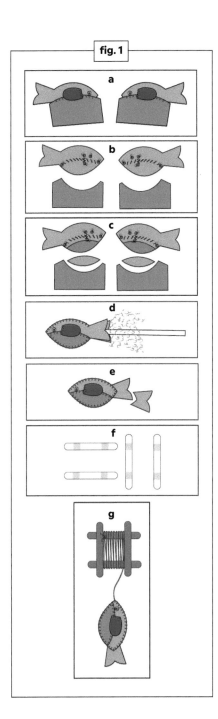

fig. 1

a

b

c

d

e

f

g

Assemble the fish

1. Thread a needle with one strand of floss (thread) to match the belly (light blue) and make a starting knot at one end. Attach the curved belly pieces to the body pieces (see the pattern for placement) using an edge-to-surface whipstitch (see **Basic Techniques**). Make a left and a right side **(fig. 1a)**. Next, stitch on the left and right fins and the eyes with matching floss (thread). Make all starting and ending knots on the wrong side.

2. Turn the assembled fish sides wrong side up and cut away the overhanging belly felt flush with the body **(fig. 1b)**. Then trim the body felt to reveal the belly felt beneath **(fig. 1c)**.

3. Thread two needles—one with floss (thread) to match the body and the other to match the belly—and individually knot their ends. Place the fish sides with wrong sides together, then whipstitch the fish sides with their matching floss (thread) colors, leaving the tail open.

4. Stuff the fish through the tail hole **(fig. 1d)**, then cut off one tail piece and discard **(fig. 1e)**. Use an edge-to-surface whipstitch with matching floss (thread) to close the hole.

Assemble the drop line

1. Using a small utility knife and ruler, cut the toothpick to length using the drop line template as a guide. Sand the ends round.

2. Lay two dropline pieces parallel (vertically) on your work surface, and the remaining two horizontally on top **(fig.1f)**. Glue the pieces together one at a time, clamping the glue joints as you go with wonder clips. Allow the glue to dry completely.

Connect the fish and line

Thread a needle with one strand of floss (thread) approx. 80cm (32in) in a color of your choice and knot one end. Stitch through the pointed nose of the fish, popping the starting knot below the surface. Make a few stitches at the nose for strength. Then remove the needle and tie the opposite end of the floss (thread) to the drop line **(fig. 1g)**. Now wrap the line and go fishing!

Galoshes

Spending so much time outdoors means that waterproof boots are an essential, especially when they're a cheerful color.

YOU WILL NEED

- Red felt (galoshes), 8 x 11cm (3¼ x 4¼in)
- Dark teal felt (soles), 4 x 4cm (1½ x 1½in)
- Chipboard (sole stabilizer), 4 x 4cm (1½ x 1½in)
- 6-stranded embroidery floss (thread), 1 skein in red
- Basic sewing kit (see **Tools & Materials**)

Optional: Glossy surface materials

- Ballpoint pen or 1cm (⅜in) diameter dowel, 15–20cm (6–8in) long
- Tube of acrylic paint (color of your choice)
- Fine-grit sandpaper or an emery board
- Clear nail polish

To make the galoshes

1. Thread a needle with one strand of matching floss (thread) and make a starting knot at one end. Fold one of the felt boot pieces in half **(fig. 1a)**. For *visible stitching* on the front seam, whipstitch with the starting and ending knots hidden between the folds of the felt **(fig. 1b)**. For an *invisible seam*, make the starting and ending knots on the stitching side, then use needle-nosed pliers to push the toe end up through the boot tube, turning it right side out.

2. Center and glue the chipboard sole stabilizer onto the felt sole. Fill the boot's leg with stuffing temporarily to keep it open as you attach the sole. Whipstitch the insole to the boot opening **(fig. 1c)**.

3. Glue the rectangle of contrasting color felt to the bottom of the boot **(fig. 1d)**. Allow it to dry, then trim around the boot, flush with the sides of the sole. Repeat on the other boot. If you plan to paint a glossy finish, wait to apply the sole felt until *after* those steps.

Glossy finish (optional)

1. Fill the boots with stuffing to hold their shape and use a brush to apply hairspray to the outside surface of the boots. Leave to dry upright on tinfoil. When completely dry and stiffened, smooth the front seam, sides, and bottom with a hot iron.

2. Remove the stuffing and insert the dowel into the boot to help you hold it while painting. Hold the dowel and press down on the sole with one finger to keep it still as you paint.

3. Using a small flat brush, apply acrylic paint directly out of the tube. Leave the boots on the dowel and turn them upside down in a cup to dry completely. Sand the surface smooth, apply a second coat of paint, and allow it to dry.

4. When dry, sand lightly again and apply a coat of clear nail polish to the surface. Allow the polish to dry completely and apply a second coat as necessary for a super-glossy finish.

5. Glue the rectangles of contrasting color felt to the bottom of the boots. Allow to dry, then trim around the boot, flush with the sides of the sole.

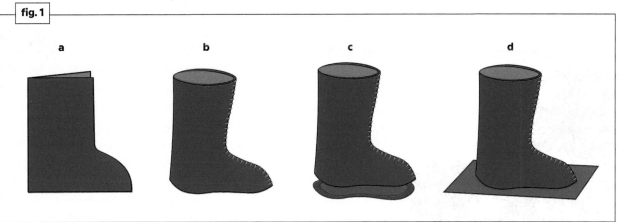

fig. 1

a   b   c   d

Wingback Chair

Badger adores his favorite armchair, whether he's reading the newspaper, relaxing after lunch, or discussing important plans with friends.

YOU WILL NEED

- Teal felt* (inner chair), 20 x 17cm (8 x 6¾in)
- Dark teal felt* (outer chair), 20 x 17cm (8 x 6¾in)
- Heather-brown felt (legs), 14 x 9cm (5½ x 3½in)
- 6-stranded embroidery floss (thread), 1 skein in mid-tone teal between the two felt colors, and 1 skein in a matching brown
- Chipboard 21 x 11cm (8¼ x 4½in)
- Wool stuffing
- Felting needle, size 38
- Foam-core or corrugated cardboard, approx. 8 x 8cm (3 x 3in)
- Basic sewing kit (see **Tools & Materials**)
- Five-minute epoxy or shoe glue

Choose two felt colors of similar tones, or the same color. Sharply contrasting colors make thread-matching difficult.

Making the sides & back

Before you begin, note that on the outside pattern pieces the seam allowance all the way around the central shaded (chipboard) areas is *not* even. This is intentional and important to the construction of the chair.

1. Before removing the paper pattern pieces from the outside felt pieces (dark teal), poke holes at the corners of the shaded area on each piece. Use a pencil to mark the corner points onto the felt— these will become registration marks for gluing the chipboard accurately. After marking, remove the paper pattern pieces from the felt.

2. Before attaching the chipboard to the chair's outer-back pieces (dark teal), cut a small rectangle from scrap chipboard to use as a glue-spreading tool. Apply tacky glue to one side of the chipboard (glue and place each piece separately), spreading in a thin, even layer so that the glue will not soak through the felt **(fig. 1a)**.

3. Using the corner pencil markings for accurate placement, position the chipboard pieces, glue side down, on the felt **(fig. 1a)** to match the pattern's seam allowances.

fig. 1

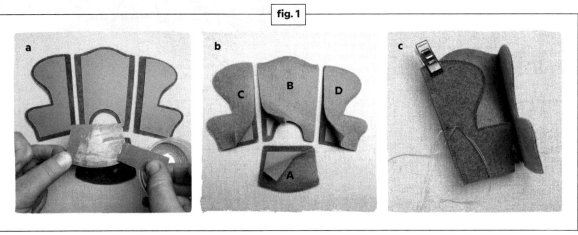

fig. 2

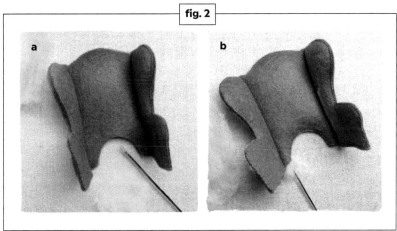

4. Thread your needle with one strand of floss (thread) and make a starting knot at one end for the following connections **(fig. 1b)**:

Seat A: Lay the two seat layers together with the chipboard between. Match the sides, and whipstitch the front edge only, hiding the starting and ending knots between the felt layers.

Back B: Lay the two center-back layers together with the chipboard between. Match the sides, and whipstitch the top edge only, hiding the knots again.

Left wing C: Lay the two wing-arm layers together with the chipboard between. Match the sides, and whipstitch the curved wing/arm edge, hiding the knots.

Right wing D: Repeat the process above on the opposite wing.

5. Thread your needle with two strands of floss (thread) and make a starting knot at one end. Whipstitch the wings to the center back one at a time, catching all four layers of felt with each stitch **(fig. 1c)**. Hide the knots.

Stuffing the upper wings & back

1. Use the bottom access hole to stuff the upper wings and upper back **(fig. 2a)**. Add enough stuffing to create volume but avoid overstuffing, or the inner seam allowances will shrink up, making the seat connection difficult.

2. Thread your needle with a single strand of floss (thread) and knot one end. Whipstitch the back's arch, leaving its left- and right-hand base open. Using a stuffing fork or skewer, finish stuffing the lower portion of the chair's back through the narrow access holes **(fig. 2b)**.

Stuffing the arms & attaching the seat

1. Thread your needle with two strands of floss (thread) and make a starting knot at one end. Whipstitch the first side of the seat to the bottom side of one arm, leaving the last quarter of the seam open for stuffing **(fig. 3a)**. Make sure you catch all four layers of felt with each stitch. Stuff the lower half of the arm through the opening, then complete the whipstitch to the back corner of the chair.

2. Repeat on the opposite side. As you close the chair box on the second seat seam, stitching will become slightly awkward as you don't have the flexibility to match the entire length of the seam while stitching. Take your time, stitching through the seat edge and arm edge separately, catching all four layers of felt with each stitch.

3. Thread your needle with two strands of floss (thread) and make a starting knot at one end. Whipstitch the access holes on either side of the back arch to the back side of the seat **(fig. 3b)**. Finally, stuff the seat **(fig. 3c)**, and whipstitch the center back seat hole closed **(fig. 3d)**.

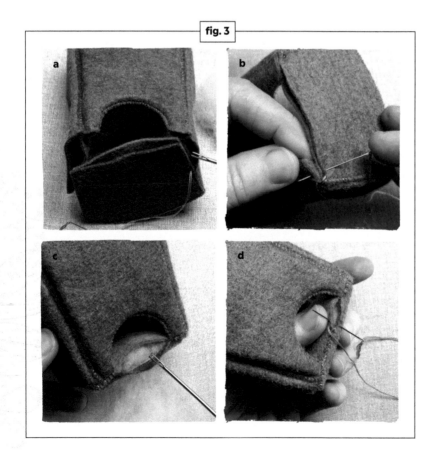

fig. 3

If you prefer to sew the legs on, skip the leg caps and hairspray (for now). Position the legs as described in step 6. Thread a needle with two strands of floss (thread) and knot one end. Use a blind stitch (see Basic Techniques) to attach the legs one leg at a time. Be patient; the rigid bottom of the chair makes stitching somewhat awkward. You may need needle-nosed pliers to pick up the point of the needle with each stitch. When all legs are attached, brush hairspray onto the chair bottom and each leg to strengthen and stiffen the legs.

fig. 4

a

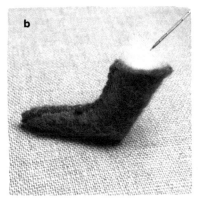

b

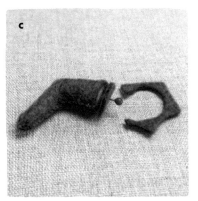

c

d

e

If you want to get extra fancy and paint a pattern on the chair, apply hairspray to the sides and back, allow it to dry, then press with a hot iron to smooth the dried surfaces. With the surface prepared, you can create your pattern design with acrylic paint or paint pens!

Making & attaching the legs

1. Thread a needle with a single strand of brown floss (thread) and knot one end. Fold the two front and two back leg pieces in half, basting (tacking) them to avoid shifting. Whipstitch the curved edge of each leg, leaving the flat top side open (**fig. 4a**). Hide the starting and ending knots.

2. Stuff the legs firmly, all the way to the end of each leg tube. The stuffing might want to spring out a bit as it fills. Use a felting needle to pierce the springy fibers (**fig. 4b**), compressing the stuffing's surface until it flattens. Trim any rogue fibers with scissors.

3. Pin a leg cap to the top of each leg, with a small overhang all the way round. Trim the caps to the size of the oval openings (**fig. 4c**). Then thread your needle with a single strand of matching brown floss (thread) and make a starting knot at one end. Whipstitch around the cap, catching the top of the leg and the cap with each stitch (**fig. 4d**).

4. Push four pins vertically through a small piece of foam-core or corrugated cardboard. Press one leg, cap side down, onto each pin. Brush the legs and bottom of the chair with non-aerosol hairspray to saturate their surfaces with the liquid (**fig. 4e**). Allow them to dry completely before moving on.

5. When the legs and chair bottom have dried and hardened, heat an iron to high. Press the cap and sides of each leg onto the iron's surface to smooth and flatten each cap, then repeat on the bottom surface of the chair.

6. Use clear five-minute epoxy or shoe glue (extra-strong contact cement used for shoes) to glue the legs to the bottom corners of the chair. Position the taller front legs with their feet pointing left and right. For the back legs, position their feet directly backward to support the weight of the chair. Sit the chair in an upside-down position and allow the glue to dry completely.

Notebooks

Not only does Ratty like to recite poetry, but he loves writing it too. Make a whole bookshelf of these little notebooks to keep him busy.

YOU WILL NEED

- 2 Sheets of US Letter (A4) printer paper

- 2 popsicle (lolly) sticks

- Felt, colored paper, leather, or other material to cover the book

- Basic sewing kit (see **Tools & Materials**)

Before you begin

Measurements are not too important in this project, as books come in so many sizes. The instructions that follow make two 1:12 scale books that can be cut to different sizes. The books pictured range from 3 x 4cm (1⅛ x 1½in) down to 2.2 x 3.3cm (⅞ x 1¼in).

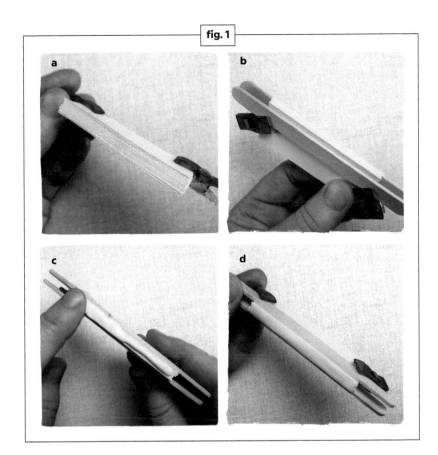

fig. 1

a

b

c

d

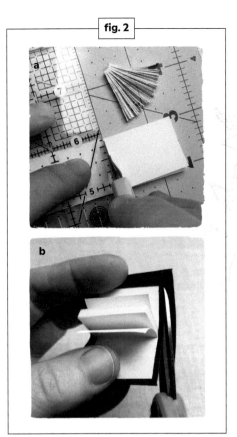

fig. 2

a

b

Prepare the paper

1. Layer the two sheets of printer paper together and fold them in half *twice* lengthwise.

2. Using a ruler, cutting mat, and utility knife, cut down the center of the folded layers of paper, then separate the pieces. This will create six folded strips and two unfolded strips. Discard the unfolded strips.

3. Separate and align the strips along their folded side. Cut the strips in half width-wise to get 12 folded pieces that are half their original length. Repeat this one more time to get 24 folded strips that are shorter than the length of your popsicle (lolly) sticks. This size will make two books, 24 folded sheets thick.

Assemble & trim the book block

1 Align the folded edges by tapping them on a flat surface, then hold the bundle together (top and bottom) with wonder clips (**fig. 1a**).

2 Place popsicle (lolly) sticks 3mm (⅛in) down on either side of the aligned, folded edges (**fig. 1b**).

3 Run a bead of tacky glue along the edge and smooth it into a thick, even layer (**fig. 1c**). Allow the glue to dry. Once dry, remove the wonder clips and popsicle (lolly) sticks (**fig.1d**).

4 Trim up the three unglued edges to the size of your choice (**fig. 2a**).

5 Glue the outside of the book block to the book cover material with the first and last pages open flat. Before the glue has dried, trim the cover with a narrow margin around the white pages (**fig. 2b**), set the books under weights (full-sized books work well), and allow the glue to dry.

6. Create book labels with fine liner pens and scraps of paper.

Slippers

Although it's Badger who likes to wear his dressing gown with them, any of the animals would appreciate a pair of these sweet little felt slippers.

YOU WILL NEED

- Top, color 1 (red felt), 3 x 6cm (1.5 x 2½in)

- Insole, color 2 (green felt), 2 x 6cm (¾ x 2½in)

- Sole, color 3 (teal felt), 2 x 6cm (1.25 x 2¾in)

- 6-strand floss (embroidery thread) in one shade to match the top color felt, and one to contrast

- Chipboard (sole stabilizer), 2 x 6cm (¾ x 2½in)

- Basic sewing kit (see **Basic Techniques**)

To make the top

1. To stitch the right and left slipper darts on the top slipper pieces (**fig. 1a**), thread your needle with a single strand of matching floss (thread) and make a starting knot at one end. Stitch each dart from the base of the V (**A**) to the edge of the slipper (**B**). Make starting and ending knots on the same sides (now the wrong sides). Make the ending knots away from the toe edges to avoid catching them in the side seams later (see **Basic Techniques**).

2. Turn the slipper tops to their right sides and push out the curve of each dart. Thread a needle with two strands of your contrast floss (thread) and knot one end. On each piece, begin with the knot on the wrong side of the felt, slightly away from the edge. Work buttonhole stitch along each curved edge opposite the dart (**fig. 1b**). Make the ending knot on the wrong side, slightly away from the edge.

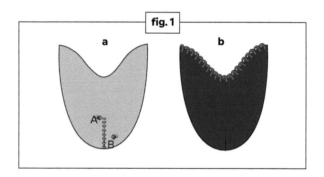

fig. 1

a   b

A
B

To make the sole

1. Center and glue the chipboard oval to the insole of the shoe (**fig. 2a**). Using the dotted line on the insole pattern piece as a reference, trim off a portion of the felt edge flush with the chipboard (**fig. 2b**).

2. Center and glue the shoe sole to the trimmed insole, with the chipboard sandwiched between the layers of felt (**fig. 2c**).

Connect the top and sole

1. Match the front of the sole (trimmed end) with the front of the top and use a wonder clip to hold the layers together (**fig. 3**).

2. To stitch the layers together, thread your needle with two strands of floss (thread), matching the top color for invisible stitches or using a contrast color for visible stitches, and make a starting knot at one end. Work either running stitch or buttonhole stitch around the slipper edge. Catch the edge of the top and sole around the sides and front of the slipper, then the sole and insole around the back. Repeat on the second slipper.

Fancy a foot pillow? Use the same Buttonhole Stitch to connect two rectangles. Leave a hole for stuffing, stuff, and close the opening with buttonhole stitch. Make a few tufting stitches through the pillow from front to back, then knot off with a square knot (right over left, then left over right). Voilà!

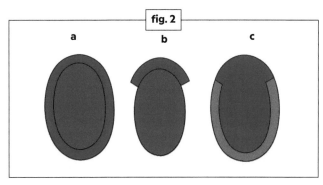

fig. 2

a   b   c

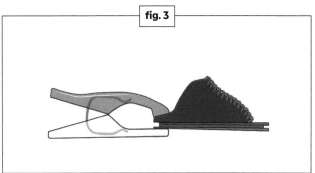

fig. 3

Basic Techniques

From threading your needle to adding the final details, the techniques you need to make the projects in this book are easy when you know how. Refer back to this section for step-by-step guidance and lots of helpful hints and tips.

Starting & Finishing

Preparing the floss (thread)

Each length of embroidery floss is composed of six individual strands, clustered together and slightly twisted. The strands need to be separated before stitching, and my kits and patterns typically suggest using either one to two strands at a time for sewing (the number needed depends on the use and the desired stitch thickness).

Separate the threads at one end, pulling only one strand at a time from the cluster of six (otherwise the strands will tangle) (**fig. 1**). If you need two or more strands for stitching, pull them individually, then ply them back together for sewing. This process removes a slight twist from the strand and makes it less likely to tangle as you stitch.

Threading the needle

If you are new to threading needles, or have been frustrated by the process in the past, you might like these two techniques. They both work well for even the smallest of needle eyes.

TECHNIQUE ONE: REVERSE THREADING

1. Make a clean cut on the thread end with sharp scissors. Then wet the cut end.

2. Pinch the end of the thread between your thumb and index finger. Pull it down between the pads of your fingers so that the end is just visible and fully gripped and supported by the fingers (not flopping around).

3. Wet the eye of the needle (fresh water or a little saliva both work well). Guide the needle's eye over the thread end (**fig. 2**), shifting the needle back and forth (along its length) to help feed the thread through the eye. Release the needle and pull the thread through.

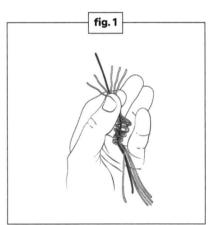

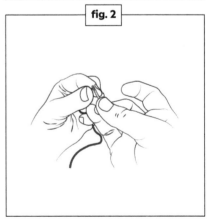

If you are a leftie, you can view the illustrations in reverse by holding a small mirror to the side of them. The reflected image will show the correct hand position for you.

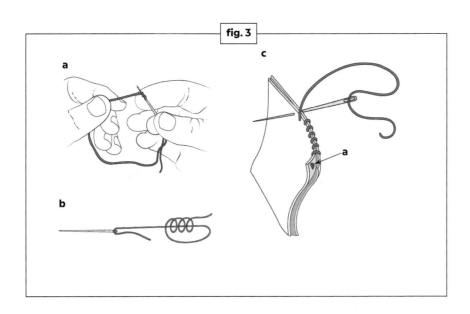

fig. 3

TECHNIQUE TWO: WAXING AND THREAD

1. Begin with step 1 of the Reverse Threading technique, cutting and wetting the thread.

2. Draw the freshly cut end through a piece of tailor's wax (or a wax tealight) to coat the fibers. Smooth, flatten, and remove excess wax from the thread by pulling it through pinched fingers/fingernails. This creates a smooth, flop-resistant end and bonds the fibers together. Now, thread the needle with my reverse threading technique or whichever method you prefer.

Starting knot

All hand-stitching starts with a knot to secure the end of the thread in the fabric. You can use any technique to make a starting knot at one end, but this one, known as a quilter's knot, creates a clean, organized knot that you will love once you get the hang of it.

It is formed by spiraling thread around the needle, then pulling the needle through the spiral. It may seem like there are many steps, but it will become second nature! The following instructions feature the right hand as the dominant hand. If you are left-handed, begin with the needle in your left hand.

1. Thread the needle and pinch the eye with the thumb and middle finger of your right hand.

2. Place the sharp end of the needle on the pad of the index finger.

3. Lift the sharp end of the needle (resting on your index finger) briefly to place the tail end of the thread beneath the needle. Put pressure on the thread end, so that it does not slip.

4. Holding the loose length of floss (thread) in your left hand between your thumb and index finger, wrap the thread over and behind the needle 1–3 times (**fig. 3a**); more wraps form a more substantial knot.

5. Finally, pinch the wrapped thread on the needle, then push up from the eye (to expose enough needle to pull from) and pull the needle up through the wraps (**fig. 3b** illustrates the way a quilting knot is formed).

TO HIDE A STARTING KNOT

Between felt layers

Sometimes your whipstitch will be visible on the outside of the piece (such as the animal's legs and torso). In this case (**fig. 3c**), hide the starting knot between the felt layers (**A**) as you begin your seam. If you are making a part (like a head) that will eventually be turned right side out to hide visible stitching, leave starting knots on the stitched side.

Inside a 3D object

To hide a starting knot inside a head (or another 3D object), pierce the object and exit a short distance away, where you want to begin your stitch. Pop the starting knot through the felt surface to lodge it in the interior stuffing.

Ending knot (knot off)

Avoid all your hard work unraveling by making a knot at the end of every seam line. Again, you can use your own technique, or if you are just learning, this trick will place the knot snuggly at the fabric's surface for a strong seam ending.

1. Make a loose overhand knot and lay the open thread loop flat on the fabric's surface.

2. Place a pin through the loop's center into the point where the thread exits the fabric. Gently pull the thread horizontally, closing the loop (**fig. 4a**). As the loop tightens, the pin secures the knot's final location and allows it to form right at the fabric's surface.

TO HIDE AN ENDING KNOT

This will make your finished creation look its best. It can be used on 3D objects like bodies and heads by piercing the needle through felt (and stuffing) to hide the knot inside the object. It also works with a single layer of felt, such as clothing. For single layers, slip the needle horizontally through the felt's surface (rather than piercing).

Pull back the knot to reveal the tiny hole beneath it. Insert the sharp end of the needle into the hole (**fig. 4b**) and exit a short distance away. Pull the needle and thread to pop the knot through the hole.

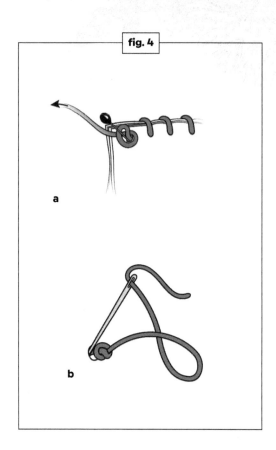

fig. 4

a

b

Stitching

Whipstitch

Whipstitch, like its name, whips or wraps around the edge of a seam, and is the main stitch used to construct our animals and clothing. When used to join two layers of felt together, standard whipstitch is made in one motion (**fig. 5a**). But because the basic stitch is so versatile, I've come up with two main variations that I call "hybrid whipstitches".

FLAT EDGE-TO-SURFACE WHIPSTITCH

This version attaches two flat pieces of felt together, one on top of another, such as pockets and patches. Each "whip" wraps around the edge of the pocket and passes through the surface felt below it. The stitch is made in two motions:

Motion 1: Back to front, catching the edge of the pocket or patch (**fig. 5b**).

Motion 2: Front to back, skimming the pocket/patch's edge and passing only through the felt below (**fig. 5c**).

3D EDGE-TO-SURFACE WHIPSTITCH

This version attaches a piece of felt at a vertical angle to a 3D shape, such as an ear. So if you don't want to glue ears, this is a great technique to know! Begin by popping the starting knot through the felt (see **Hiding a Starting Knot Inside a 3D Object**) and exiting the needle at the corner of the ear. Each stitch is then made in two motions:

Motion 1: Just below the ear (**fig. 5d**), insert the needle through the head's surface at **A**, using a small scooping action.

Motion 2: Reverse directions, passing the needle through the edge of the ear. Repeat actions 1 and 2 to continue the stitch line and attach the ear to the head. Remove pins as you progress with the seam. When the ear is attached, knot off and hide your ending knot.

SECURING LIMBS

Without some stitching finesse, securing legs and arms may be awkward! The process is made smooth by sharply angling the needle (**fig. 5e**) rather than working with the needle perpendicular to the seam.

Make each stitch with one motion by passing the needle through the limb and out the edge of the body. As you work, make adjustments, bending limbs for easier access to the seam.

There are many ways to adapt whipstitch for different applications. If the version you're using feels awkward, consider how you might tweak it to create a variation you enjoy using.

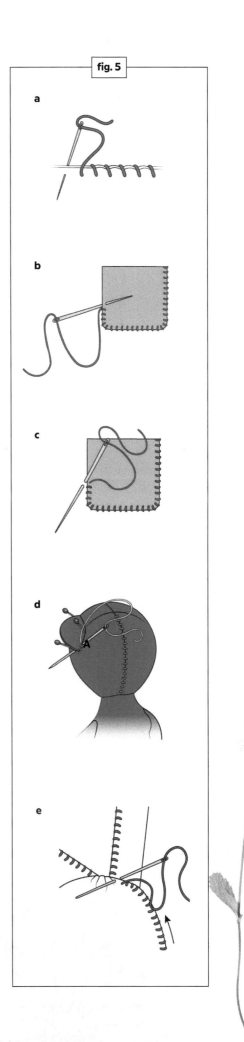

fig. 5

a

b

c

d

e

Running stitch & basting (tacking) stitch

These stitches are not only very simple, but are both essentially the same stitch! Depending on their purpose—functional or temporary—only the length of the stitch changes.

RUNNING STITCH

This stitch consists of small, evenly spaced stitches that look like a dashed line (**fig. 6a**). It's often used in this book to create the borders of jackets and sleeves (such as Ratty's pea coat, Mole's blazer, Toad's tailcoat, and Badger's dressing gown). For evenly spaced stitches, make each one using two motions: front to back, then back to front (as opposed to scooping each stitch in one movement).

BASTING (TACKING) STITCH

These are long, temporary running stitches used instead of pins or wonder clips. You can also use them to attach paper patterns to felt for cutting, if you have no washi tape or iron-on patterns to hand.

Backstitch

The backstitch is a versatile stitch that makes a solid stitching line without spacing gaps. It can be used decoratively or as a durable connecting stitch. In fact, it is the strongest stitch you can make without a sewing machine!

To make a backstitch, begin by threading your needle with a single or double strand of floss/thread (depending on the application) and make a starting knot at one end. Enter the fabric from back to front at the start of your stitch line, and make one stitch forward from front to back (in an appropriate length to the scale of your project).

Motion 1: Back to front: enter the needle two stitch lengths forward.

Motion 2: Front to back: insert the point of the needle one stitch length backward to touch the end of the previous stitch (**fig. 6b**).

Motion 3: Repeat steps 1 and 2 to make a line of backstitches.

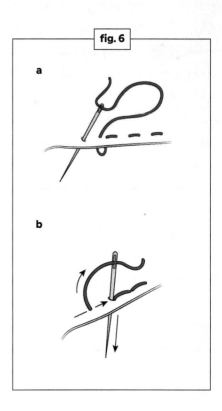

fig. 6

a

b

Bar tack

To hold just one point in place, use a bar tack. Make one running stitch forward (ending on the under-side of the work), then make the second stitch in a backward motion, coming up at the starting point. Make the second stitch over the first, then continue by making several stitches over the top of each other to create a strong point of connection. Knot off on the back side of the work.

Knots know-how

No matter which stitch you are using, unwanted knots can happen. Here is my advice for avoiding them (for as long as possible!), plus a reason to stay optimistic when you do get one.

Avoiding knots: The working thread between your seamline and needle will naturally build up a twist as you stitch. By regularly "dropping" the needle and thread to let the twist spin out, you can avoid many pesky knots and dramatically increase your stitching enjoyment!

Most knots are slip knots: Some knots are inevitable. The good news is, the majority will be slip knots! When you come across a knot in your working thread, inspect it. It will usually look like a loop, leaning in one direction or the other. Using the working needle (or a straight pin) as your tool, insert the point through the loop and pull it in the opposite direction from which it was leaning. You might even hear a tiny "pop". Then pull the thread on either side of the loop (simultaneously outward) to pull out the slip knot.

Blind stitch

This invisible stitch is made from outside the work and is used for attaching heads and tails. Use *two strands* of floss (thread) to ensure a secure attachment.

1. Insert the needle through the head (or tail) parallel with the seam line. Then switch to the opposite side—the neck (or body)—and take another parallel stitch.

2. Stitch back and forth between the two sides, as shown (**fig. 7**). After every few stitches, pull the thread snugly to draw the two sides together. The felt edge will turn inward as the thread is tightened, and the stitches will disappear.

3. Continue like this twice around for strength, then secure with an ending knot.

French knot

A purely decorative little stitch that forms organized ballshaped knots (used as details on the back of Toad's tailcoat). This stitch is hard to fully demonstrate with illustrations because there really is a "feel" to getting the knot just right and positioned snug to the surface. I recommend watching a few videos and practicing on scrap pieces of felt to perfect it.

1. To make the stitch, bring the needle up from the back of the work to the front (**fig. 8a** *red dot*) and wrap the thread around the shaft of the needle three times. To form the knot, the wraps on the needle must be within the loop of the working thread.

2. Take the tip of the needle back to where it first came up and insert it back into the fabric (**fig. 8b**). To form the knot, pull the needle through the wrapped thread to the back side of the work (**fig. 8c**).

3. Come up again to form the next knot in exactly the same way.

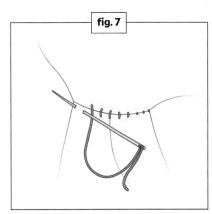

fig. 7

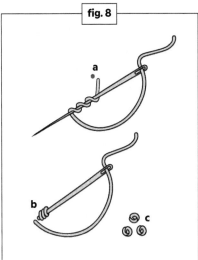

fig. 8

The size of the knot can be made larger or smaller. Increase or reduce either the number of wraps around the needle or the number of strands used.

Lazy daisy stitch

The decorative petal-like shape of lazy daisy stitch (**fig. 9**) can be made individually, or in groups to form flowers (used on the back of Toad's tailcoat).

1. Begin by coming up from the back of the fabric to the front.

2. Then insert the needle down through the fabric just next to where the thread came out in step 1 and bring it up a short distance away. This distance will become the length of your daisy petal. Before pulling the needle and thread through, loop the thread around the needle's point (**fig. 9a**).

3. Now pull the thread all the way through, then insert the needle as shown in **fig. 9b**. to create a small stitch that locks the crest of the loop to the surface. Repeat to make more petals in any orientation you like.

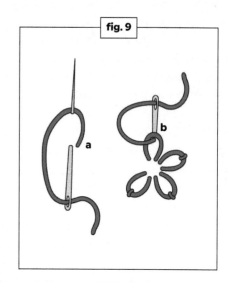

fig. 9

Satin stitch

Another variation on the whipstitch, this time the stitches whip in front and behind a surface, stacking one after the other to fill a shape. You might prefer to use a satin stitch (**fig. 10**) as an alternative to painted noses, as suggested in Ratty's chapter.

1. Lightly sketch the nose shape on the face with a pencil. Thread a needle with two strands of floss (thread) and make an ending knot.

2. Hide the starting knot beneath the felt surface (see **Hiding knots**) and exit the needle in the upper left-hand corner of the nose outline.

3. Move the needle in a backward motion and enter its point in the upper right-hand corner of the nose outline. Pass the needle through the felt (beneath the surface) exiting just below the first sating stitch on the left-hand side.

4. Continue making stitches in this manner so that they fill the space, lying smoothly across the surface, each one parallel to the previous stitch. Avoid pulling or cinching the stitches, or the nose may appear pinched.

fig. 10

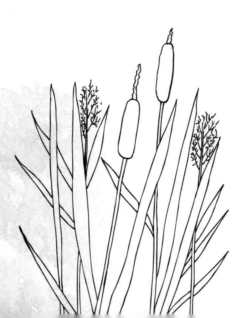

Buttonhole stitch

Although it looks similar to a blanket stitch, the buttonhole stitch is superior in strength and practicality! Both stitches bind the edge of fabric, but the buttonhole stitch has a nifty feature of locking down each stitch as it forms with a twist in the thread. This maintains tension for easy stitching and a neat finish. Some makers prefer the buttonhole stitch to the whipstitch for connecting regular seams. It is used in this book as a sturdy interior edging for buttonholes or a decorative finish on an outer edge such as Mole's cap and the Picnic Blanket.

1. Enter the needle through the felt edge as though you were making a whipstitch. Before the thread tightens around the edge, pass the needle through the back of the loop at (**fig. 11a**) to form a twist as shown at (**fig. 11b**).

2. Continue pulling the thread through until the twist reduces to a bump or "purl" on the fabric's edge (**fig. 11c**).

MANAGING YOUR THREAD

Buttonhole stitch uses a lot of thread, so it is good to know how to seamlessly change to a new piece. Avoid letting your thread become too short before changing. Buttonhole stitches get fussier as the working thread shortens and are more likely to tangle.

To end a thread

Insert the needle into the edge of the felt (**fig. 11d**) just beyond the final locking purl, so that the thread is not visible on either side. Exit a short distance away, then make and hide an ending knot (see **To Hide an Ending Knot**).

To join a new thread

Thread the needle with a new length of thread and make a starting knot at one end. Enter the needle through the felt's surface only, exiting before the last locking purl (**fig. 11e**). Pop the starting knot through to hide it beneath the surface and continue as before.

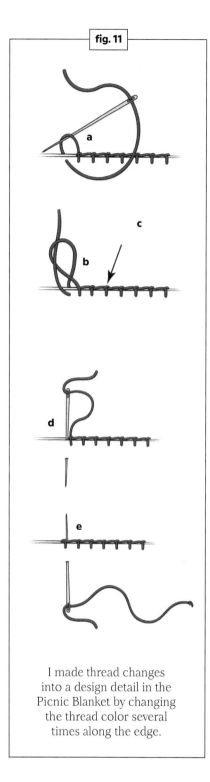

fig. 11

I made thread changes into a design detail in the Picnic Blanket by changing the thread color several times along the edge.

Basic Techniques

117

Construction Tips & Tricks

Using darts

A dart is a V-shaped cut in a flat pattern that, when stitched together, creates volume. In our full-scale world, darts are commonly found in clothes such as a woman's fitted top, where they make way for busts and curves. In this book, the darts on the side-head pieces help form the rounded shape at the back of the skull. On Badger, they help to shape his squarish muzzle.

To stitch darts, pinch the V and match its sides together, then stitch from the base of the V to the outer edge. On the tiny muzzle darts of Badger, keep the stitches close together and use the Setting Back Knots technique to move the ending knots away from the edge.

Setting back knots

Sometimes, your needle will hit a starting or ending knot from another seam and get stuck in it as you stitch. Because I know certain knots could become a nuisance later on, I set them back from the edge. For example, when stitching the darts on a side-head piece, knots left at the edge are likely to catch as you sew the head's center seam. It is hard to explain everywhere this might happen, but as you experience it, you can make a note and use this trick!

To do so, after making the last stitch of a seam, and before making your knot, insert the needle through the felt's surface to move the exit point away from the end of the seam (**fig. 12**). Make the ending knot here and hide it beneath the surface as necessary.

Stitching strong seams

Strong seams are important when stitching and stuffing our animals, avoiding holes and general weaknesses.

SEAM ALLOWANCE

A depth of approx. 1.5mm (1⁄16in) is the perfect seam allowance for our small-scale projects (and as such is already included in the patterns). When stitching seams, make each stitch through the edge of the felt, entering at **A** and exiting at **B**, catching equal amounts of felt on either side (**fig. 13a**). The arrow from **C** to **D** illustrates a weak seam (**fig. 13b**).

WHIPSTITCH TENSION

Another element of making a durable seam is stitch tension. As you complete each whipstitch, give the thread a tug to tighten it around the seam. Not so hard that the floss threatens to break, but just enough tension that it pulls snugly in around the seam. **Fig. 14** illustrates the slight indentation of the stitches in the seam edge with good tension.

SEAMS AND STUFFING

Although strong seams are desirable everywhere, they are particularly important on the animals' heads. Unless otherwise stated, the heads are intended to be firmly packed with stuffing. This stretches out seams and adds fullness and dimension to the animal's heads. Synthetic and bamboo felt are not as strong as wool, so the resulting seams will be slightly weaker. As a result, heads made from those materials should not be filled as firmly.

STUFFING THE HEAD

It is surprising how much stuffing you can pack into a small space. The shape and density of the head is important, especially when it comes to creating the face.

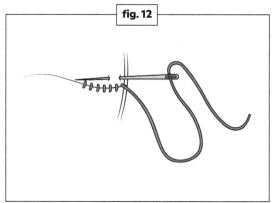

fig. 12

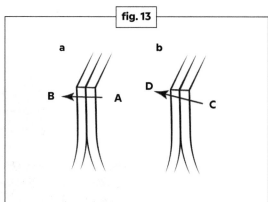

fig. 13

a   b

B ← A   D ← C

TARGETED STUFFING

Targeted stuffing can be added in two ways, with either the scissor channel technique or by sliding stuffing between the core of wool and the felt's surface. Think of this process as sculpting from the inside out. Once the head appears nearly full, add stuffing to targeted areas to subtly increase their volume. Targeted stuffing refines the head shape—for example, adding more fiber to the cheeks to plump them or adding volume to the back of the head if it is not symmetrical.

CUTTING A SCISSOR CHANNEL

Try inserting your scissors (through the neck hole) into the center of the packed wool fiber and snipping an interior pathway. By cutting a hole into which you can add more wool, you can plump the head from its center. This same cutting technique is used to create a channel for the pipe cleaner that protrudes from the neck of the body, and when attaching heads to bodies.

Holding your work

The way you hold your stitching as you work is just as important as all the other techniques. It can make the process easier and more precise, which in turn makes it much more enjoyable!

STITCH DIRECTION

Try stitching from your body outward (away from you) for more control of your stitches. This way, your thread will hang down over the completed stitches, rather than interfering with the stitches ahead (**fig. 14**).

HANDS-ON EXPERIENCE

The way you hold the work as you stitch (along with practice) will help you make evenly sized and spaced stitches. Hold the work in your left hand, lightly pinched between your thumb and ring finger and your index finger and middle finger (**fig. 15**). This position will help support the edge that you're stitching and allow you to tilt the work back and forth with each stitch so that you can see the entrance (**A**) and exit (**B**) of each stitch.

Practice make perfect

Why not make an extra head to practice your stitches, stitch tension, and stuffing if you have time? Pack the head tightly to see the strength of your stitches. Are they all holding? Is the tension even throughout the seam? Can you firmly fill the head without any stitches pulling through the felt edge? Practice packing the stuffing so that the head proportions are even and don't appear lopsided. What can you do to make it better on the real thing? After you've done some practicing, feel confident with your stitching and stuffing, cut open the sample, and reuse the filling. No need to waste beautiful wool stuffing!

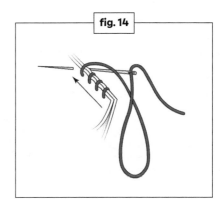

fig. 14

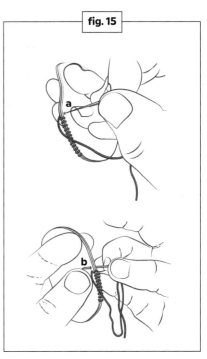

fig. 15

Patterns

How to use the patterns:

· To ensure you fit all your pattern pieces onto each piece of felt, I have provided handy pattern-layout diagrams for each animal. These show how I positioned my patterns on the different pieces of felt in the You Will Need lists. The layouts will also help you ensure you have gathered all the templates you need for your chosen character and outfit.

· All the patterns you need to create the characters are in this section, including an additional set for dollhouse-scale animals. At the end, there are also patterns for the accessories.

· Refer to the Pattern Key to identify what the different lines and marks mean.

· Printable versions of the patterns are also available to download at full size from www.bookmarkedhub.com. They are available in both A4 and US letter size.

PATTERN KEY (all animals):

Fold line	-------------------
Outline cut line	━━━━━━
Interior cut line	··········
Running stitch border	- - - - - - -
Placement marking	▬▬▬
Cut out interior shape	⬚

Pattern Layout: Mole (not to scale)

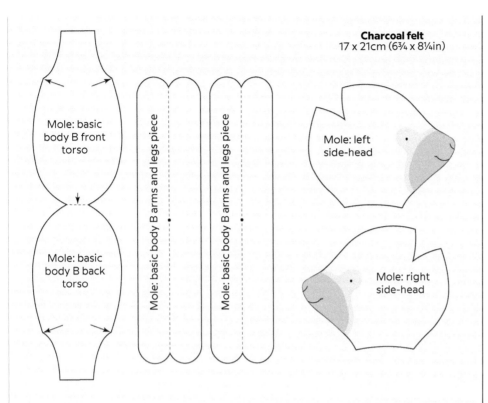

Teal felt
5 x 4cm (2 x 1½in)

Mole: pants pocket

Mole: collar band

Mole: cap form

Charcoal felt
17 x 21cm (6¾ x 8¼in)

Mole: basic body B front torso

Mole: basic body B back torso

Mole: basic body B arms and legs piece

Mole: basic body B arms and legs piece

Mole: left side-head

Mole: right side-head

Pumpkin felt
5 x 2cm (2 x ¾in)

Mole: cap band

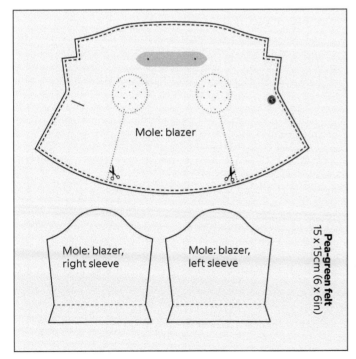

Mole: blazer

Mole: blazer, right sleeve

Mole: blazer, left sleeve

Pea-green felt
15 x 15cm (6 x 6in)

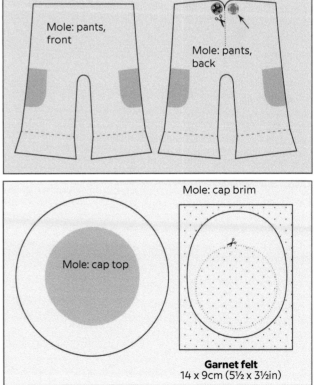

Carrot-orange felt
14 x 9cm (5½ x 3½in)

Mole: pants, front

Mole: pants, back

Mole: cap brim

Mole: cap top

Garnet felt
14 x 9cm (5½ x 3½in)

Pattern Layout: Ratty (not to scale)

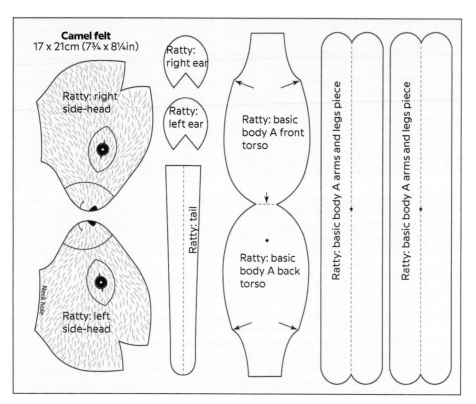

Camel felt
17 x 21cm (7¾ x 8¼in)

Ratty: right side-head

Ratty: right ear

Ratty: left ear

Ratty: basic body A front torso

Ratty: basic body A arms and legs piece

Ratty: basic body A arms and legs piece

Ratty: tail

Ratty: basic body A back torso

Neck hole

Ratty: left side-head

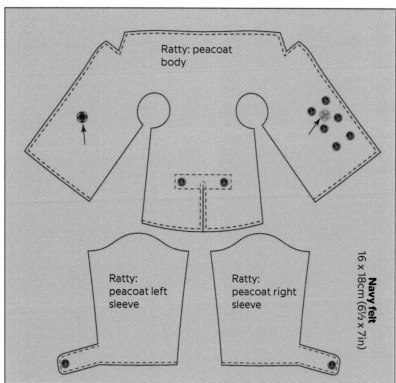

Ratty: peacoat body

Ratty: peacoat left sleeve

Ratty: peacoat right sleeve

Navy felt
16 x 18cm (6½ x 7in)

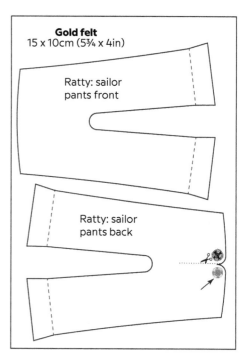

Gold felt
15 x 10cm (5¾ x 4in)

Ratty: sailor pants front

Ratty: sailor pants back

Ratty: cravat

Red felt
13 x 24.5cm (5 x 9½in)

Pattern Layout: Badger (not to scale)

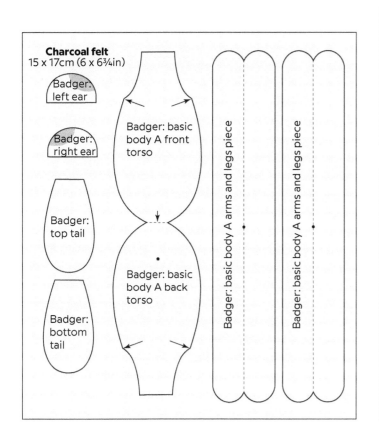

Charcoal felt
15 x 17cm (6 x 6¾in)

Badger: left ear

Badger: right ear

Badger: top tail

Badger: bottom tail

Badger: basic body A front torso

Badger: basic body A back torso

Badger: basic body A arms and legs piece

Badger: basic body A arms and legs piece

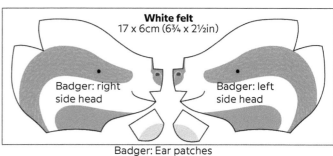

White felt
17 x 6cm (6¾ x 2½in)

Badger: right side head

Badger: left side head

Badger: Ear patches

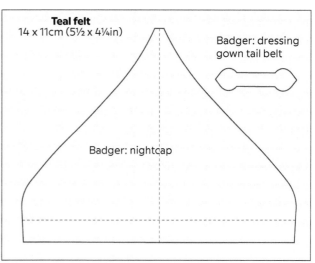

Teal felt
14 x 11cm (5½ x 4¼in)

Badger: dressing gown tail belt

Badger: nightcap

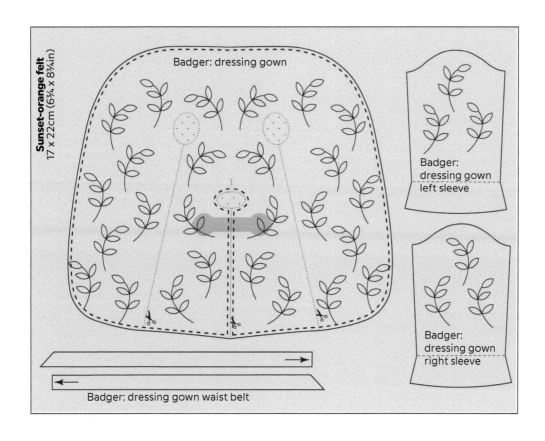

Sunset-orange felt
17 x 22cm (6¾ x 8¾in)

Badger: dressing gown

Badger: dressing gown left sleeve

Badger: dressing gown right sleeve

Badger: dressing gown waist belt

Pattern Layout: Toad (not to scale)

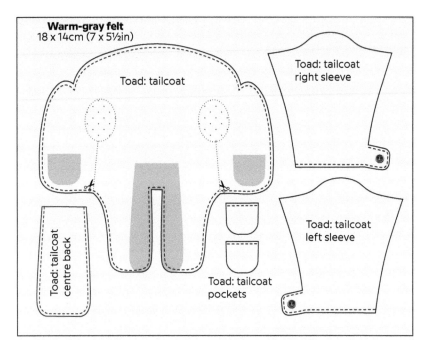

Warm-gray felt
18 x 14cm (7 x 5½in)

Toad: tailcoat

Toad: tailcoat right sleeve

Toad: tailcoat centre back

Toad: tailcoat pockets

Toad: tailcoat left sleeve

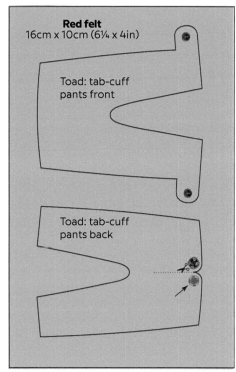

Red felt
16cm x 10cm (6¼ x 4in)

Toad: tab-cuff pants front

Toad: tab-cuff pants back

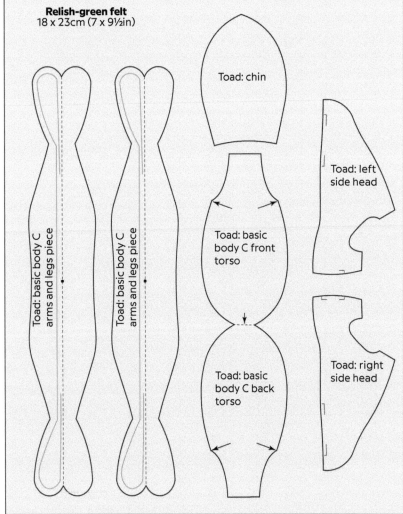

Relish-green felt
18 x 23cm (7 x 9½in)

Toad: chin

Toad: basic body C arms and legs piece

Toad: basic body C arms and legs piece

Toad: left side head

Toad: basic body C front torso

Toad: right side head

Toad: basic body C back torso

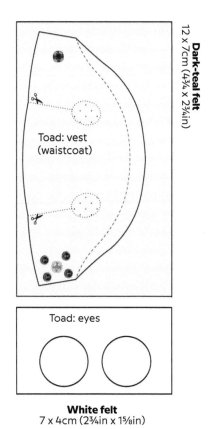

Dark-teal felt
12 x 7cm (4¾ x 2¾in)

Toad: vest (waistcoat)

Toad: eyes

White felt
7 x 4cm (2¾in x 1⅝in)

Templates

Refer to **Before You Begin: Transferring Patterns** before cutting the patterns. Cut all the paper patterns before cutting the felt. Cut felt in single layers for accuracy.

BODY, ARMS, & LEGS

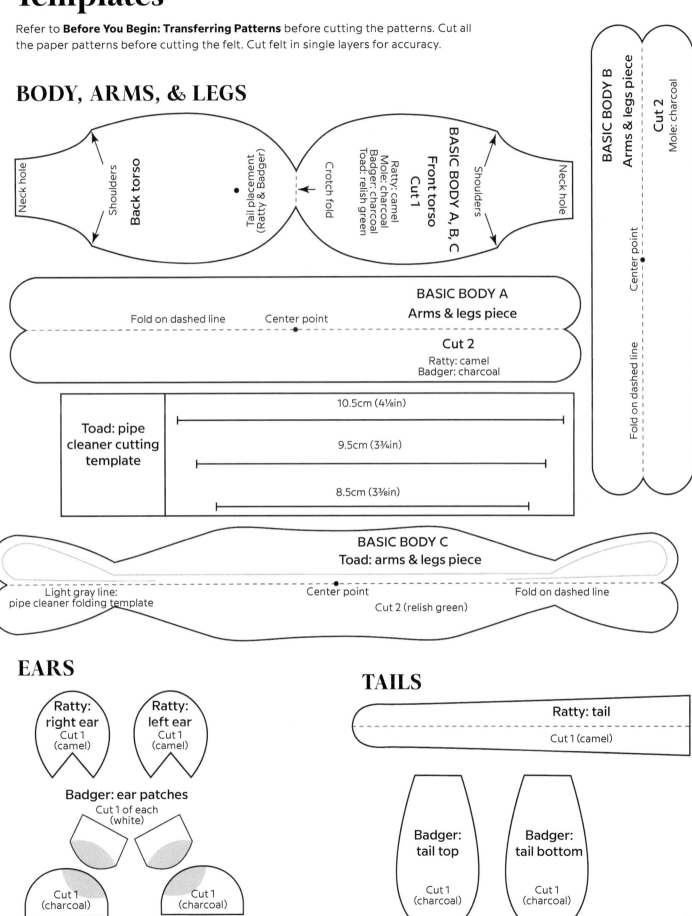

Back torso

Neck hole

Shoulders

Tail placement (Ratty & Badger)

Crotch fold

BASIC BODY A, B, C
Front torso
Cut 1
Ratty: camel
Mole: charcoal
Badger: charcoal
Toad: relish green

Shoulders

Neck hole

BASIC BODY B
Arms & legs piece
Cut 2
Mole: charcoal

Center point

Fold on dashed line

BASIC BODY A
Arms & legs piece

Fold on dashed line   Center point

Cut 2
Ratty: camel
Badger: charcoal

Toad: pipe cleaner cutting template

10.5cm (4⅛in)

9.5cm (3¾in)

8.5cm (3⅜in)

BASIC BODY C
Toad: arms & legs piece

Light gray line: pipe cleaner folding template

Center point

Fold on dashed line

Cut 2 (relish green)

EARS

Ratty: right ear
Cut 1 (camel)

Ratty: left ear
Cut 1 (camel)

Badger: ear patches
Cut 1 of each (white)

Cut 1 (charcoal)

Cut 1 (charcoal)

Badger: left ear   Badger: right ear

TAILS

Ratty: tail
Cut 1 (camel)

Badger: tail top
Cut 1 (charcoal)

Badger: tail bottom
Cut 1 (charcoal)

125

HEADS

Ratty

Ratty: right side-head
(with painted features)
Cut 1 (camel)

Neck hole

Ratty: left side-head
(with painted features)
Cut 1 (camel)

Neck hole

Mole

Mole: right side-head
(with painted features)
Cut 1 (charcoal)

Neck hole

Mole: left side-head
(with painted features)
Cut 1 (charcoal)

Neck hole

Badger

Badger: right side-head
(with painted features)
Cut 1 (white)

Neck hole

Badger: left side-head
(with painted features)
Cut 1 (white)

Neck hole

Patterns

Toad

Toad: left eye
Cut 1 (white)

Toad: right eye
Cut 1 (white)

Front

Front

Toad: left side-head
Cut 1 (relish green)

Center seam

Toad: right side-head
Cut 1 (relish green)

Center seam

Toad: chin
Cut 1 (relish green)

Neck hole

126

RATTY: PEACOAT

TOAD: TAILCOAT & VEST (WAISTCOAT)

Ratty: peacoat
left sleeve

Cut 1 (navy)

Ratty: peacoat
right sleeve

Cut 1 (navy)

Toad: vest
(waistcoat)

Cut 1 (dark teal)

Collar fold

Ratty: cravat   Cut 1 (red)

Attach snap last,
after fitting the
coat

Ratty: belt

Cut 1 (navy)

Ratty: peacoat body

Cut 1 (navy)

Patterns

Attach snap
on opposite
side of felt

Toad: tailcoat
right sleeve

Cut 1 (warm gray)

Toad:
tailcoat right
pocket

Cut 1
(warm
gray)

Cut 1
(warm
gray)

Toad: tailcoat
left pocket

Toad:
tailcoat
center-
back

Cut 1
(warm
gray)

Pocket
placement

Center-back tail placement

Pocket
placement

Cut 1 (warm gray)

Toad: tailcoat

Toad: tailcoat
left sleeve

Cut 1 (warm gray)

127

RATTY: SAILOR PANTS

MOLE: PANTS

TOAD: TAB-CUFF PANTS

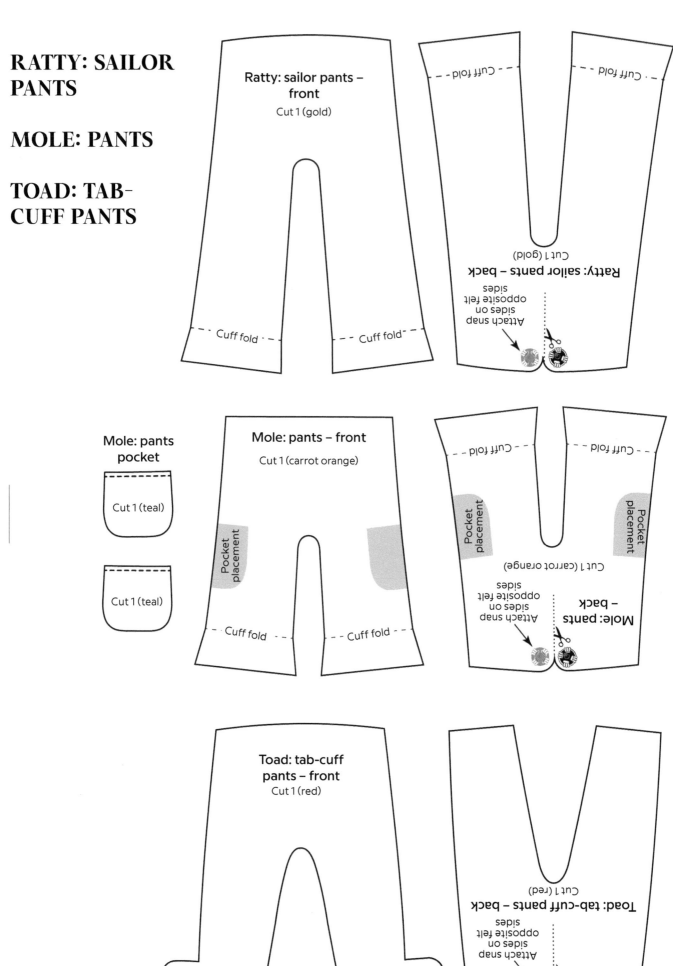

Ratty: sailor pants – front
Cut 1 (gold)

Cuff fold — — Cuff fold

Cuff fold — — Cuff fold

Ratty: sailor pants – back
Cut 1 (gold)

Attach snap on opposite felt sides

Mole: pants pocket

Cut 1 (teal)

Cut 1 (teal)

Mole: pants – front
Cut 1 (carrot orange)

Pocket placement

Cuff fold — — Cuff fold

Cuff fold — — Cuff fold

Pocket placement

Pocket placement

Mole: pants – back
Cut 1 (carrot orange)

Attach snap on opposite felt sides

Toad: tab-cuff pants – front
Cut 1 (red)

Toad: tab-cuff pants – back
Cut 1 (red)

Attach snap on opposite felt sides

Patterns

128

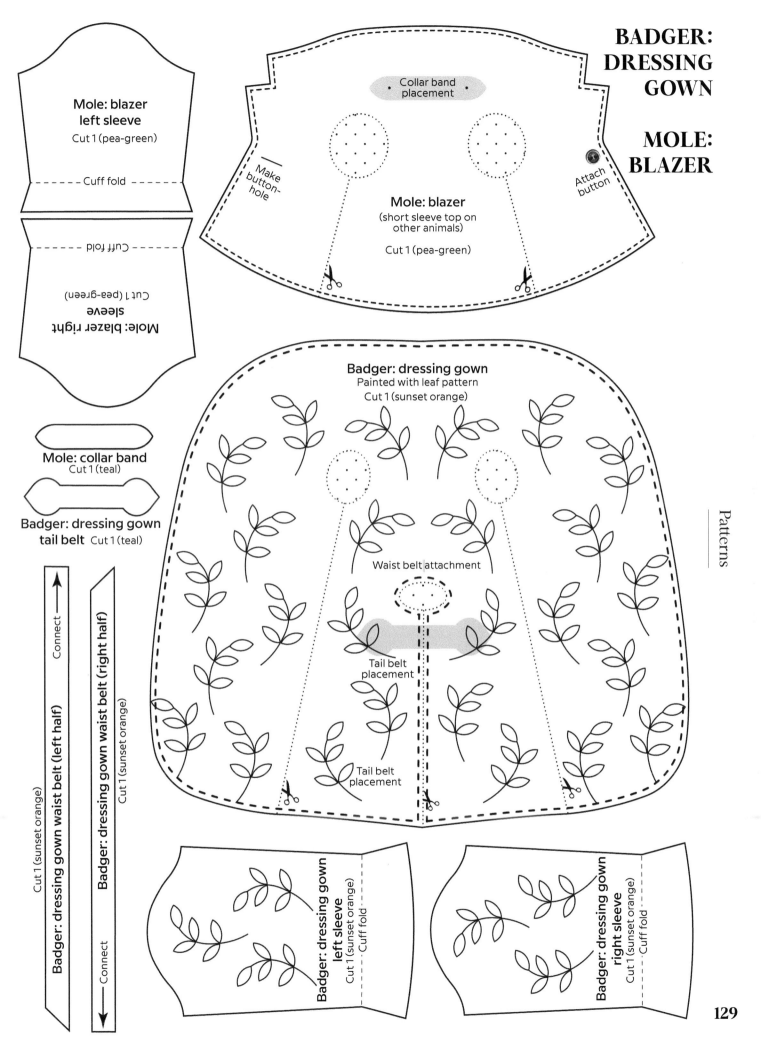

Mole: blazer
left sleeve
Cut 1 (pea-green)

- - - Cuff fold - - -

- - - Cuff fold - - -

Mole: blazer right
sleeve
Cut 1 (pea-green)

Mole: collar band
Cut 1 (teal)

Badger: dressing gown
tail belt Cut 1 (teal)

Collar band
placement

Make
button-
hole

Attach
button

Mole: blazer
(short sleeve top on
other animals)
Cut 1 (pea-green)

BADGER:
DRESSING
GOWN

MOLE:
BLAZER

Patterns

Badger: dressing gown
Painted with leaf pattern
Cut 1 (sunset orange)

Waist belt attachment

Tail belt
placement

Tail belt
placement

Badger: dressing gown waist belt (left half)
Cut 1 (sunset orange)
Connect

Badger: dressing gown waist belt (right half)
Cut 1 (sunset orange)
Connect

Badger: dressing gown
left sleeve
Cut 1 (sunset orange)
Cuff fold

Badger: dressing gown
right sleeve
Cut 1 (sunset orange)
Cuff fold

MOLE: CAP

BADGER: NIGHTCAP

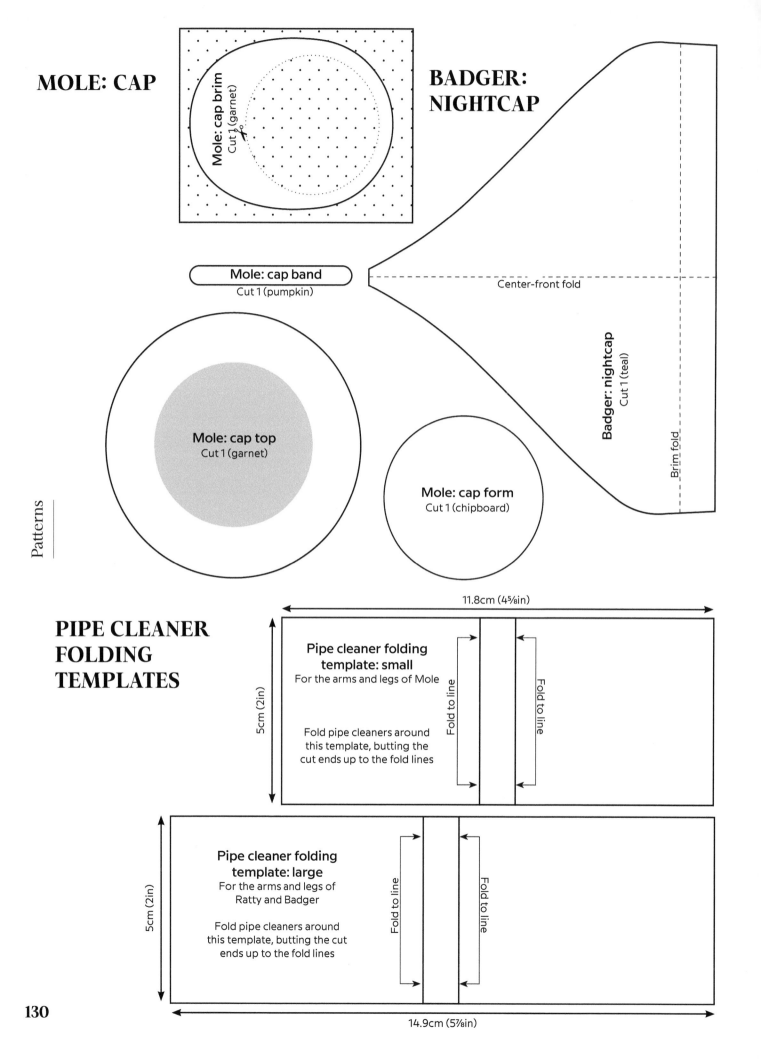

Mole: cap brim
Cut 1 (garnet)

Mole: cap band
Cut 1 (pumpkin)

Mole: cap top
Cut 1 (garnet)

Mole: cap form
Cut 1 (chipboard)

Center-front fold

Badger: nightcap
Cut 1 (teal)

Brim fold

PIPE CLEANER FOLDING TEMPLATES

11.8cm (4⅝in)

5cm (2in)

Pipe cleaner folding template: small
For the arms and legs of Mole

Fold pipe cleaners around this template, butting the cut ends up to the fold lines

Fold to line

Fold to line

5cm (2in)

Pipe cleaner folding template: large
For the arms and legs of Ratty and Badger

Fold pipe cleaners around this template, butting the cut ends up to the fold lines

Fold to line

Fold to line

14.9cm (5⅞in)

Patterns

DOLLHOUSE SCALE BODY, ARMS, & LEGS

Basic body A
Arm & legs piece

Fold on dashed line

Center point

Cut 2
Mole: charcoal

Basic body B
Arm & legs piece

Fold on dashed line

Center point

Cut 2
Ratty: camel
Badger: charcoal

Toad: pipe cleaner cutting template

8.4cm (3¼in)

7.6cm (3in)

6.8cm (2⅝in)

Basic body C
Arm & legs piece

Light gray line: pipe cleaner folding template

Center point

Cut 2
Toad: relish green

Fold on dashed line

Neck hole

Shoulders

Basic body
A, B, C
Front torso

Cut 1
Ratty: camel
Mole: charcoal
Badger: charcoal
Toad: relish green

Crotch fold

Tail placement
(Ratty & Badger)

Back torso

Shoulders

Neck hole

Patterns

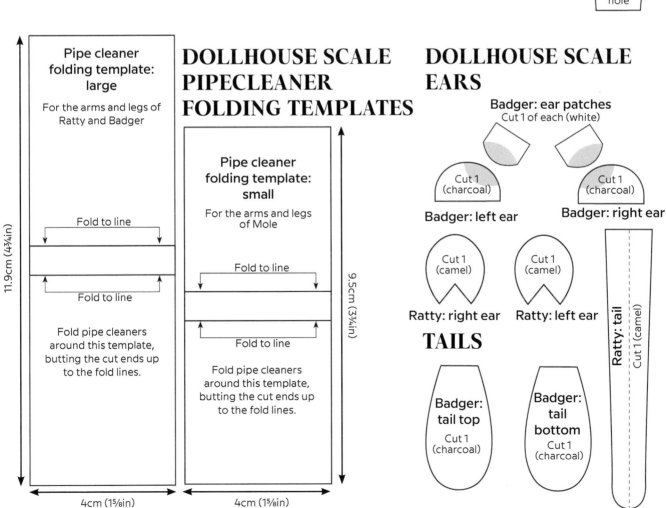

Pipe cleaner folding template: large

For the arms and legs of Ratty and Badger

11.9cm (4¾in)

Fold to line

Fold to line

Fold pipe cleaners around this template, butting the cut ends up to the fold lines.

4cm (1⅝in)

DOLLHOUSE SCALE PIPECLEANER FOLDING TEMPLATES

Pipe cleaner folding template: small

For the arms and legs of Mole

Fold to line

Fold to line

Fold pipe cleaners around this template, butting the cut ends up to the fold lines.

9.5cm (3¾in)

4cm (1⅝in)

DOLLHOUSE SCALE EARS

Badger: ear patches
Cut 1 of each (white)

Cut 1
(charcoal)

Cut 1
(charcoal)

Badger: left ear

Badger: right ear

Cut 1
(camel)

Cut 1
(camel)

Ratty: right ear

Ratty: left ear

TAILS

Badger: tail top
Cut 1
(charcoal)

Badger: tail bottom
Cut 1
(charcoal)

Ratty: tail
Cut 1 (camel)

131

DOLLHOUSE SCALE HEADS

Patterns

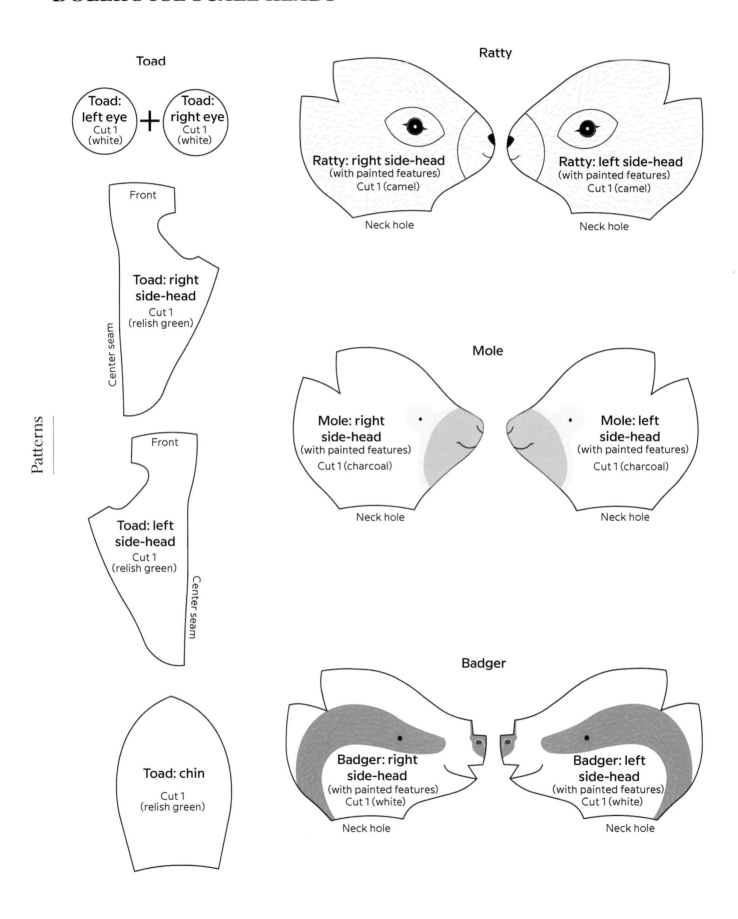

Toad

Toad:
left eye
Cut 1
(white)
+
Toad:
right eye
Cut 1
(white)

Front

Toad: right
side-head
Cut 1
(relish green)

Center seam

Front

Toad: left
side-head
Cut 1
(relish green)

Center seam

Toad: chin

Cut 1
(relish green)

Ratty

Ratty: right side-head
(with painted features)
Cut 1 (camel)

Neck hole

Ratty: left side-head
(with painted features)
Cut 1 (camel)

Neck hole

Mole

Mole: right
side-head
(with painted features)
Cut 1 (charcoal)

Neck hole

Mole: left
side-head
(with painted features)
Cut 1 (charcoal)

Neck hole

Badger

Badger: right
side-head
(with painted features)
Cut 1 (white)

Neck hole

Badger: left
side-head
(with painted features)
Cut 1 (white)

Neck hole

DOLLHOUSE SCALE

BADGER: DRESSING GOWN
MOLE: BLAZER

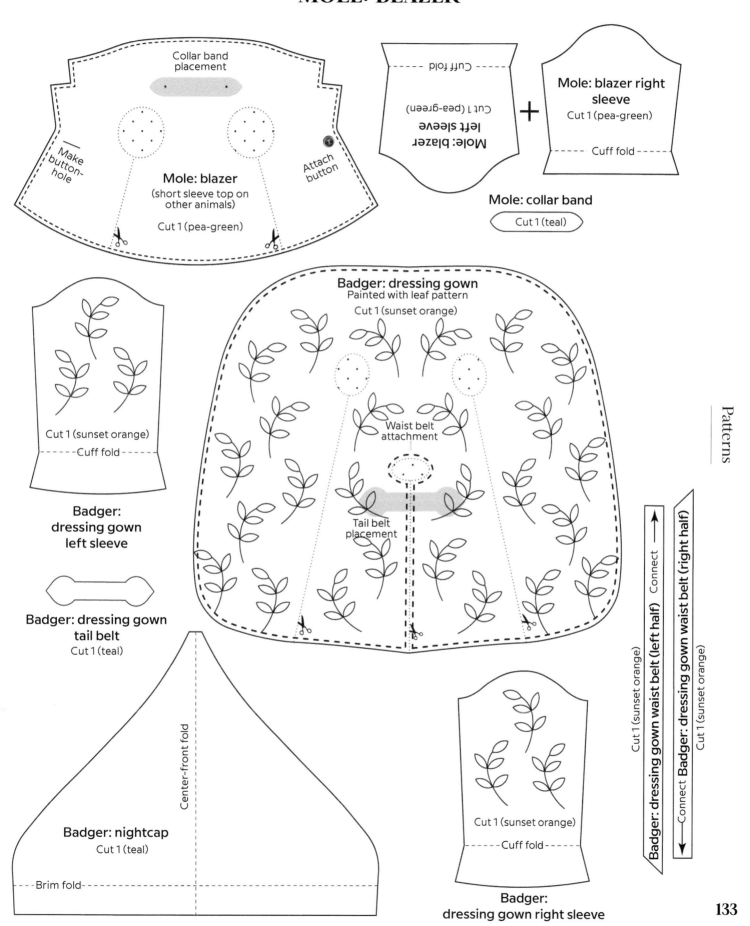

Collar band placement

Make button-hole

Mole: blazer
(short sleeve top on other animals)
Cut 1 (pea-green)

Attach button

Mole: blazer left sleeve
Cut 1 (pea-green)
Cuff fold

Mole: blazer right sleeve
Cut 1 (pea-green)
Cuff fold

Mole: collar band
Cut 1 (teal)

Badger: dressing gown
Painted with leaf pattern
Cut 1 (sunset orange)

Waist belt attachment

Tail belt placement

Cut 1 (sunset orange)
Cuff fold

Badger:
dressing gown
left sleeve

Badger: dressing gown
tail belt
Cut 1 (teal)

Center-front fold

Badger: nightcap
Cut 1 (teal)

Brim fold

Cut 1 (sunset orange)
Cuff fold

Badger:
dressing gown right sleeve

Cut 1 (sunset orange)
Badger: dressing gown waist belt (left half)

Connect

Connect Badger: dressing gown waist belt (right half)
Cut 1 (sunset orange)

DOLLHOUSE SCALE

RATTY: PEACOAT
TOAD: TAILCOAT & VEST (WAISTCOAT)

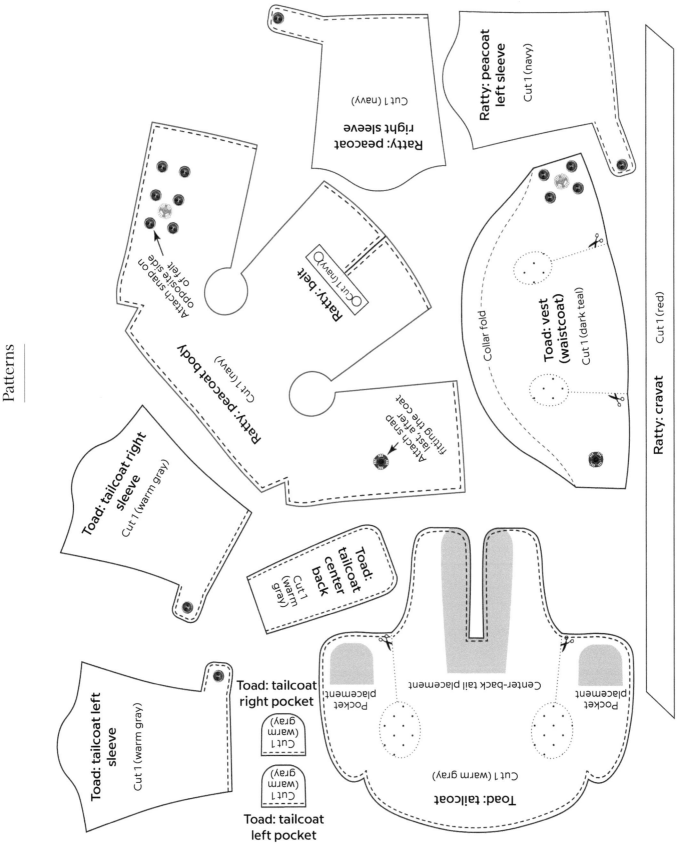

Ratty: peacoat
right sleeve
Cut 1 (navy)

Ratty: peacoat
left sleeve
Cut 1 (navy)

Attach snap on
opposite side
of felt

Ratty: peacoat body
Cut 1 (navy)

Ratty: belt
Cut 1 (navy)

Attach snap
last after
fitting the coat

Toad: vest
(waistcoat)
Cut 1 (dark teal)

Collar fold

Ratty: cravat   Cut 1 (red)

Toad: tailcoat right
sleeve
Cut 1 (warm gray)

Toad:
tailcoat
center
back
Cut 1
(warm
gray)

Toad: tailcoat left
sleeve
Cut 1 (warm gray)

Toad: tailcoat
right pocket

Cut 1
(warm
gray)

Cut 1
(warm
gray)

Toad: tailcoat
left pocket

Pocket
placement

Center-back tail placement

Pocket
placement

Toad: tailcoat
Cut 1 (warm gray)

DOLLHOUSE SCALE

RATTY: SAILOR PANTS
MOLE: PANTS & CAP
TOAD: TAB-CUFF PANTS

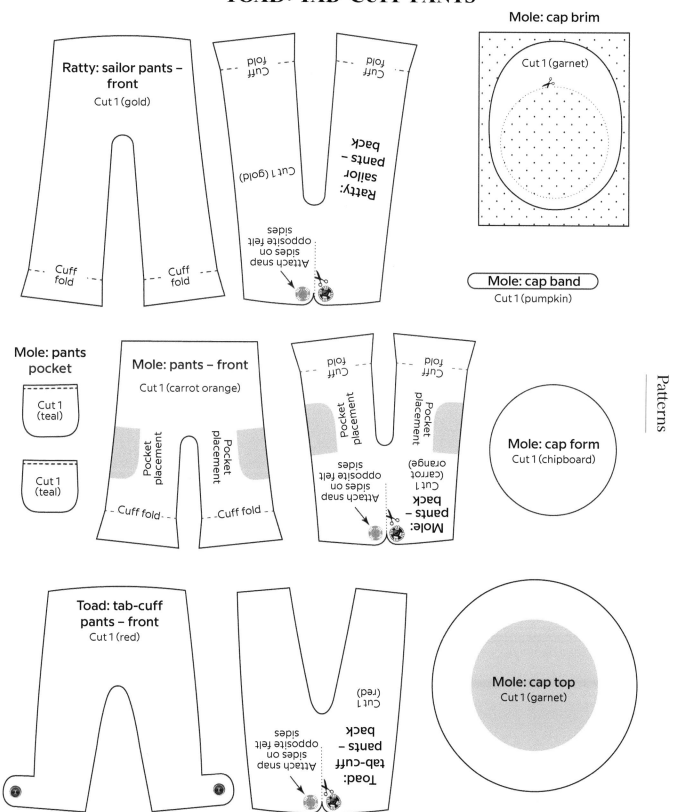

Mole: cap brim

Cut 1 (garnet)

Ratty: sailor pants – front
Cut 1 (gold)

Cuff fold

Cuff fold

Cuff fold

Cuff fold

Ratty: sailor pants – back
Cut 1 (gold)

Attach snap on opposite felt sides

Mole: cap band
Cut 1 (pumpkin)

Mole: pants pocket

Cut 1 (teal)

Cut 1 (teal)

Mole: pants – front
Cut 1 (carrot orange)

Pocket placement

Pocket placement

Cuff fold

Cuff fold

Cuff fold

Cuff fold

Pocket placement

Pocket placement

Mole: pants – back
Cut 1 (carrot orange)

Attach snap on opposite felt sides

Mole: cap form
Cut 1 (chipboard)

Toad: tab-cuff pants – front
Cut 1 (red)

Toad: tab-cuff pants – back
Cut 1 (red)

Attach snap on opposite felt sides

Mole: cap top
Cut 1 (garnet)

Patterns

135

WINGBACK CHAIR

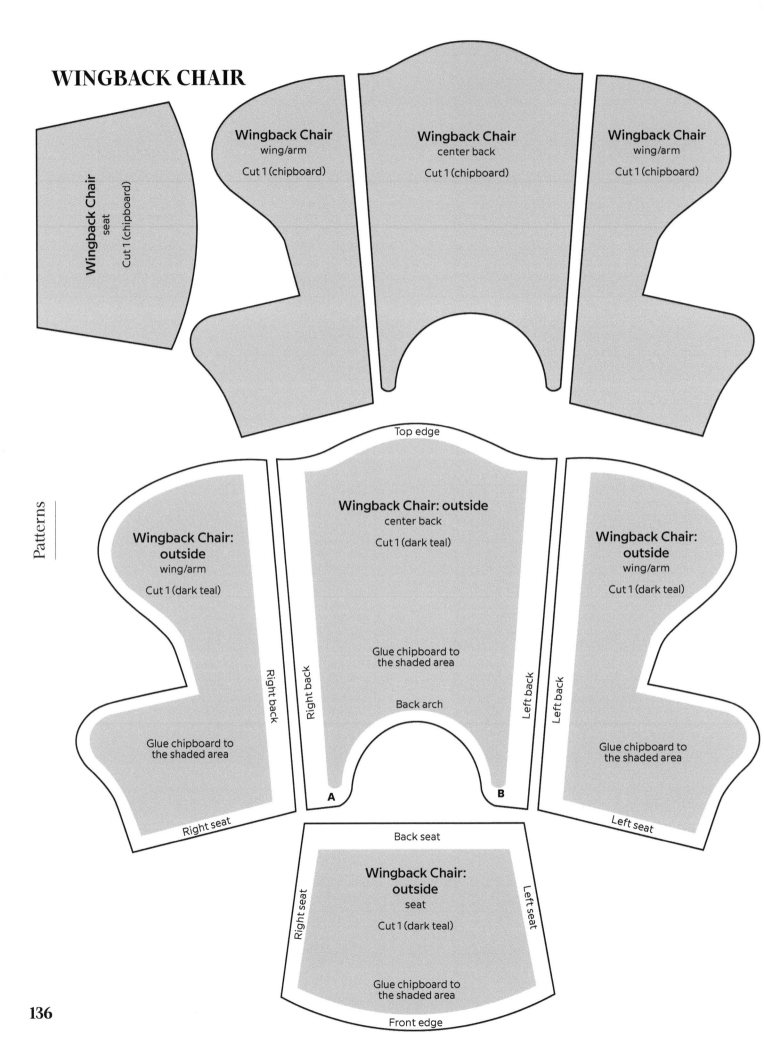

Wingback Chair
seat
Cut 1 (chipboard)

Wingback Chair
wing/arm
Cut 1 (chipboard)

Wingback Chair
center back
Cut 1 (chipboard)

Wingback Chair
wing/arm
Cut 1 (chipboard)

Patterns

Top edge

Wingback Chair: outside
wing/arm
Cut 1 (dark teal)

Glue chipboard to
the shaded area

Right seat

Wingback Chair: outside
center back
Cut 1 (dark teal)

Glue chipboard to
the shaded area

Back arch

Right back

Right back

Left back

Left back

Wingback Chair: outside
wing/arm
Cut 1 (dark teal)

Glue chipboard to
the shaded area

Left seat

A

B

Back seat

Right seat

Left seat

Wingback Chair: outside
seat
Cut 1 (dark teal)

Glue chipboard to
the shaded area

Front edge

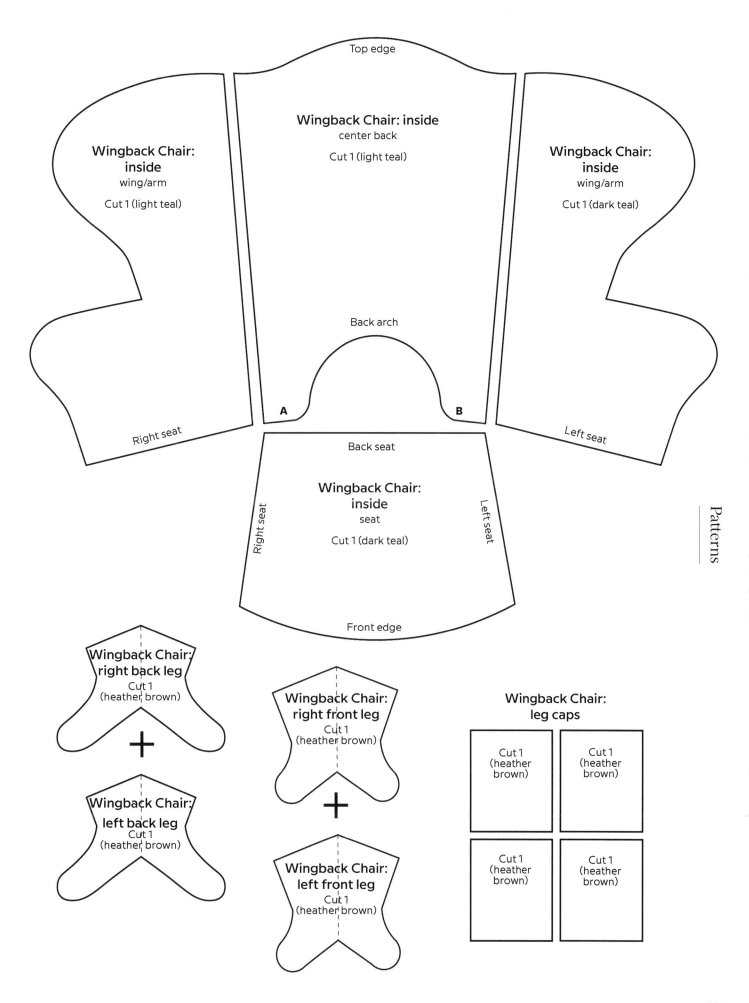

Top edge

Wingback Chair:
inside
wing/arm

Cut 1 (light teal)

Wingback Chair: inside
center back

Cut 1 (light teal)

Wingback Chair:
inside
wing/arm

Cut 1 (dark teal)

Back arch

A

B

Right seat

Left seat

Back seat

Wingback Chair:
inside
seat

Cut 1 (dark teal)

Right seat

Left seat

Front edge

Wingback Chair:
right back leg
Cut 1
(heather brown)

Wingback Chair:
left back leg
Cut 1
(heather brown)

Wingback Chair:
right front leg
Cut 1
(heather brown)

Wingback Chair:
left front leg
Cut 1
(heather brown)

Wingback Chair:
leg caps

Cut 1 (heather brown)	Cut 1 (heather brown)
Cut 1 (heather brown)	Cut 1 (heather brown)

Patterns

137

BLANKET, SLIPPERS & GALOSHES

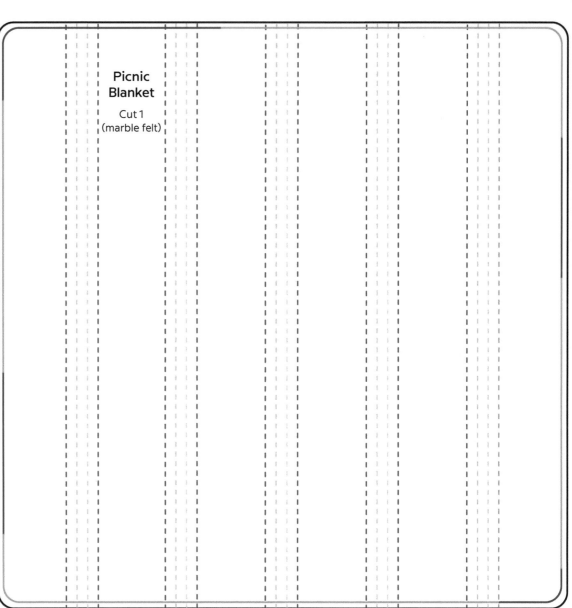

Picnic Blanket

Cut 1
(marble felt)

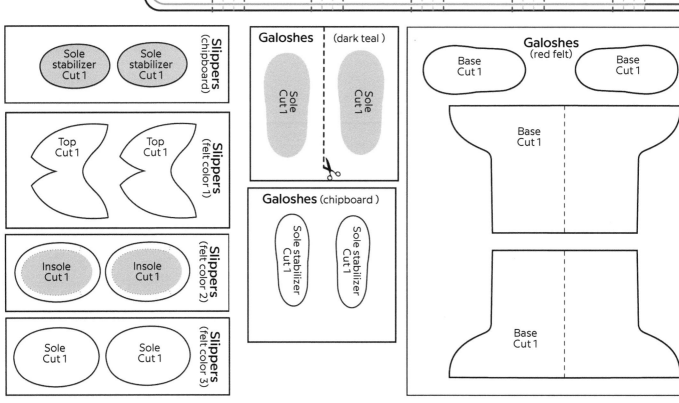

Slippers (chipboard)

Sole stabilizer Cut 1

Sole stabilizer Cut 1

Slippers (felt color 1)

Top Cut 1

Top Cut 1

Slippers (felt color 2)

Insole Cut 1

Insole Cut 1

Slippers (felt color 3)

Sole Cut 1

Sole Cut 1

Galoshes (dark teal)

Sole Cut 1

Sole Cut 1

Galoshes (chipboard)

Sole stabilizer Cut 1

Sole stabilizer Cut 1

Galoshes (red felt)

Base Cut 1

Base Cut 1

Base Cut 1

Base Cut 1

LUNCHEON BASKET & FISH

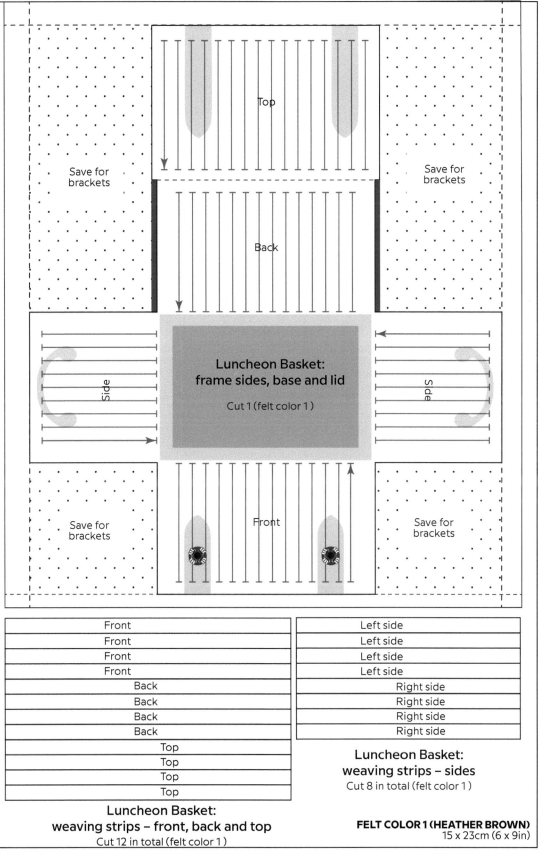

Save for brackets

Top

Back

Save for brackets

Side

**Luncheon Basket:
frame sides, base and lid**

Cut 1 (felt color 1)

Side

Save for brackets

Front

Save for brackets

**Luncheon Basket:
inside base**
Chipboard
Cut 1

CHIPBOARD 5 x 7cm (2 x 2¾in)

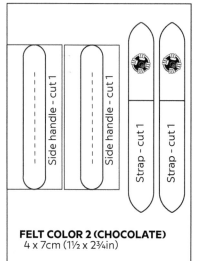

Side handle – cut 1

Side handle – cut 1

Strap – cut 1

Strap – cut 1

FELT COLOR 2 (CHOCOLATE)
4 x 7cm (1½ x 2¾in)

Front		Left side
Front		Left side
Front		Left side
Front		Left side
Back		Right side
Back		Right side
Back		Right side
Back		Right side
Top		
Top		
Top		
Top		

**Luncheon Basket:
weaving strips – sides**
Cut 8 in total (felt color 1)

**Luncheon Basket:
weaving strips – front, back and top**
Cut 12 in total (felt color 1)

FELT COLOR 1 (HEATHER BROWN)
15 x 23cm (6 x 9in)

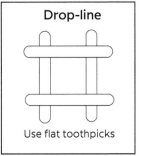

Drop-line

Use flat toothpicks

Fish: fins (pumpkin)

Cut 1

Cut 1

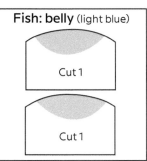

Fish: belly (light blue)

Cut 1

Cut 1

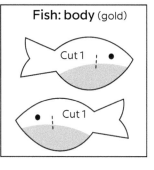

Fish: body (gold)

Cut 1

Cut 1

About the author

Although youth is fleeting, childhood stories and wistful memories endure. Kenneth Grahame knew this as he wrote the classic adventures that became *The Wind in the Willows*, and Cynthia Treen knows it as well. Her charming felt animal designs are classics in the making, with their own stories waiting to be imagined. Cynthia's passion for teaching and drafting comes through in her detailed instructions and illustrations, which are perfect for guiding beginners and advanced makers alike.

For over 25 years, Cynthia Treen has designed and taught makers everywhere in front of, and behind, the camera. From *Martha Stewart Living* magazine and TV to a PBS home and garden show, her book *Last-Minute Fabric Gifts* (2006, Stewart, Tabori & Chang), her line of *threadfollower* hand-stitching kits (2012–today), and finally to her growing community of maker friends on Patreon. Cynthia's ability to organize, illustrate, and distill projects makes them approachable and inspiring to makers of all experience levels, giving them a feeling of success and mastery.

Visit her Etsy shop at threadfollower.com, Instagram @cynthia.treen, or her threadfollower youtube channel. You can also join her growing community of friends on Patreon for exclusive monthly projects, meet-ups, and zoom workshops. On Patreon, supporters have access to her entire library of monthly projects, patterns, and video tutorials.

Find Cynthia online:

- etsy.com/shop/CynthiaTreenStudio
- instagram.com/cynthia.treen
- youtube.com/user/threadfollower
- patreon.com/ cynthiatreenstudiothreadfollower

Acknowledgments

Thank you to my fantastic team at David and Charles; you have made this entire process an absolute pleasure! Enormous thanks go to Ame, my fantastic editor, who believed in me and allowed my seed of an idea to flourish on the River Bank, Meadows, and Wild Wood of Kenneth Grahame's imagination. My gratitude goes out to Anna Wade and Lucy Waldron for their gorgeous book design. The alchemy of layering and collage have seamlessly blended old and new into something most magical. Thank you for cherry-picking my book! Enormous thanks go out to Jenny Fox-Proverbs, copy editor extraordinaire! Your humor, mind for detail, and clarity are astonishing. Thank you for every word you touched, moved, and polished. My dyslexic mind boggles at your wizardry! And thank you to Sophie Seager and Jeni Chown—I am so grateful to you both and to all who helped make this book a reality!

Thank you, Laura O'Neil, my dear friend, and Assistant? Studio Manager? It is time we came up with a proper title to express the depth of my gratitude, the breadth of all you do, and the grace of your easy spirit! Thank you, Lenore Welby. I am beyond happy to have you back in my world on the daily! How strange and wonderful that we've come full circle from MSL and my first book (thank you for that, my friend!) to working together again. You are a treasure! To Pete Mars, your friendship means the world to me! I am overwhelmed with gratitude that you offered to take on the set building for this book. It would not have been as beautiful or magical without your skills and imagination! Now, on to our next project together!

To @dawsondigsdolls, thank you for your friendship and for sharing access to your magnificent miniature prop house! To my Mom, for repeatedly saying throughout my youth, "We can make that!". To Lee and Brian for your generosity and friendship, and for sharing your home with me. My most heartfelt thanks go out to Helen for your friendship, wisdom, and kindred spirit. I look forward to many days spent bird watching and making together. To my dear heart-felt friends, Patsy, Amy, Anne, Karen, Beth, Julie, Kit, and Fran... Thank you for your inspiration, your laughter, and all your encouragement. My weeks are not complete without our days together!

Thank you to my Patreon friends for your kindness, enthusiasm, and support. I am over the moon to have you all on my team and in my inner circle! Let's keep stitching, sharing, learning, and growing together! With gratitude to my friends at the Handicrafts Club in Providence, Rhode Island (handicraftclub. org). Thank you for welcoming me with open arms and allowing me to teach with you! This one-of-a-kind club has been a haven of women's crafts education since 1904!

Karl, thank you for making the world a greener, sweeter place, for your brotherly wisdom, our morning tea & all your YouTube & insta tinkering that inspire and propel me forward! And to my dearest Karen, may your inner gold shine brilliantly, and may happiness be yours. Whatever may come, let us continue to make each other better, now and always.

Resources

BASIC TOOL KIT

Available from craft stores, sewing and notions suppliers, and etsy.com:

- Self-healing cutting mat and clear acrylic rule
- Wire cutters
- Needle nosed pliers
- Water soluble pens (fabric marker)
- Tacky glue: I use Aleene's Original Tacky Glue and Aleene's Original Fast Grab or Turbo Tacky Glue

ROTARY CUTTER

US olfa.com
Fiskars.com
UK backstitch.co.uk

EMBROIDERY NEEDLES

Tulip needles

US cynthiatreenstudio.com
benziedesign.com
purlsoho.com
knitonequilttoo.com
kimonomomo.etsy.com
UK backstitch.co.uk
coolcrafting.co.uk

LONG DARNERS

US cynthiatreenstudio.com
knitonequilttoo.com
UK coolcrafting.co.uk
merchantandmills.com

SMALL SCISSORS

I use Fiskars Razor-edge, micro-tip, easy-action 5in

International
Fiskars.com

UTILITY KNIFE

Olfa 9mm 300 Ratchet-Lock Precision Utility Knife

US olfa.com
UK olfacutters.co.uk

PINS

Short, straight, glass-head pins 28mm (1in) by Little House

US cynthiatreenstudio.com
kimonomomo.etsy.com

WONDER CLIPS

US cynthiatreenstudio.com
benziedesign.com
purlsoho.com
knitonequilttoo.com
UK backstitch.co.uk

STUFFING FORK

Barbara Willis mini stuffing fork
US cynthiatreenstudio.com
barbarawillisdesigns.com
UK etsy.com/uk/

WASHI TAPE

MT Tape
US mt-tape.us
UK mtmaskingtape.co.uk

FREEZER PAPER

US cynthiatreenstudio.com
benziedesign.com
UK backstitch.co.uk

TAILORS WAX

Merchant & Mills pure beeswax

US benziedesign.com
purlsoho.com
knitonequilttoo.com
UK coolcrafting.co.uk
merchantandmills.com

CREATIVE MATERIALS

WOOL AND RAYON BLEND FELT

US cynthiatreenstudio.com
benziedesign.com
achildsdream.com
UK backstitch.co.uk
billowfabrics.co.uk
coolcrafting.co.uk
woolfeltcompany.co.uk

DMC EMBROIDERY FLOSS

US cynthiatreenstudio.com
benziedesign.com
knitonequilttoo.com
purlsoho.com
Worldwide
dmc.com
backstitch.co.uk

100% WOOL STUFFING

US cynthiatreenstudio.com
benziedesign.com
achildsdream.com
UK backstitch.co.uk

COTTON PIPE CLEANERS

US cynthiatreenstudio.com
threadfollower.com
benziedesign.com
UK artandcraftfactory.co.uk
merchantandmills.com

SEW-IN EYES

US cynthiatreenstudio.com
Internationally
Doll- and bear-making suppliers, and etsy.com

SNAPS & MINIATURE BUTTONS

US cynthiatreenstudio.com
UK Sewing and notions suppliers, and etsy.com

SUPER DUO BEADS

Worldwide
Readily available at craft stores, and on Etsy

PAINT, PENS AND FINELINERS

US dickblick.com
UK cassart.co.uk
amazon.co.uk

The paint pens used in this book:

Uni Posca 0.7mm pin tip (white and black)

Uni Posca 0.7mm bullet tip (white and black)

Zeyar Art paint pen (olive)

Arteza acrylic marker plastic nib, fine (white and black)

PAINT BRUSH

I use a no.6 round watercolor brush

US dickblick.com
UK cassart.co.uk
amazon.co.uk

Cynthia Treen Studio

Many of the creative materials listed below can be found on the author's own website, along with her line of threadfollower kits, patterns and more.

www.cynthiatreenstudio.com

Resources

Index

A DAVID AND CHARLES BOOK
© David and Charles, Ltd 2022

David and Charles is an imprint of David and Charles, Ltd
Suite A, Tourism House, Pynes Hill, Exeter, EX2 5WS

Text and Designs © Cynthia Treen 2022
Layout and Photography © David and Charles, Ltd 2022

First published in the UK and USA in 2022

A catalogue record for this book is available from the British Library.

ISBN-13: 9781446309223 paperback
ISBN-13: 9781446381656 EPUB
ISBN-13: 9781446381649 PDF

This book has been printed on paper from approved suppliers and made from pulp from sustainable sources.

Printed by CPI Group (UK) Ltd for:
David and Charles, Ltd, Suite A, Tourism House, Pynes Hill, Exeter, EX2 5WS

Publishing Director: Ame Verso
Managing Editor: Jeni Chown
Project Editor: Jenny Fox-Proverbs
Head of Design: Anna Wade
Designer: Lucy Waldron
Pre-press Designer: Ali Stark
Illustrations: Cynthia Treen
Art Direction: Anna Wade
Styling: Cynthia Treen
Photography: Cynthia Treen and Karen Philippi
Production Manager: Beverley Richardson

David and Charles publishes high-quality books on a wide range of subjects. For more information visit www.davidandcharles.com.

Share your makes with us on social media using #dandcbooks and follow us on Facebook and Instagram by searching for @dandcbooks.

Layout of the digital edition of this book may vary depending on reader hardware and display settings.

Permission to copy

Both I and the publisher grant permission for the owner of this book to photocopy or scan the patterns within, either at 100% or scaled to a different size, for personal use.

Thank you so much, Cynthia Treen (author), David and Charles (publisher), and Ratty, Mole, Badger and of course, the amazing Mr Toad!